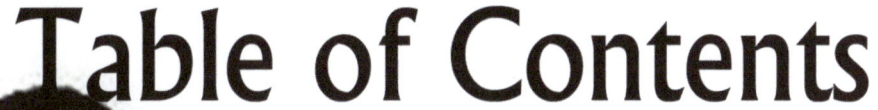

Table of Contents

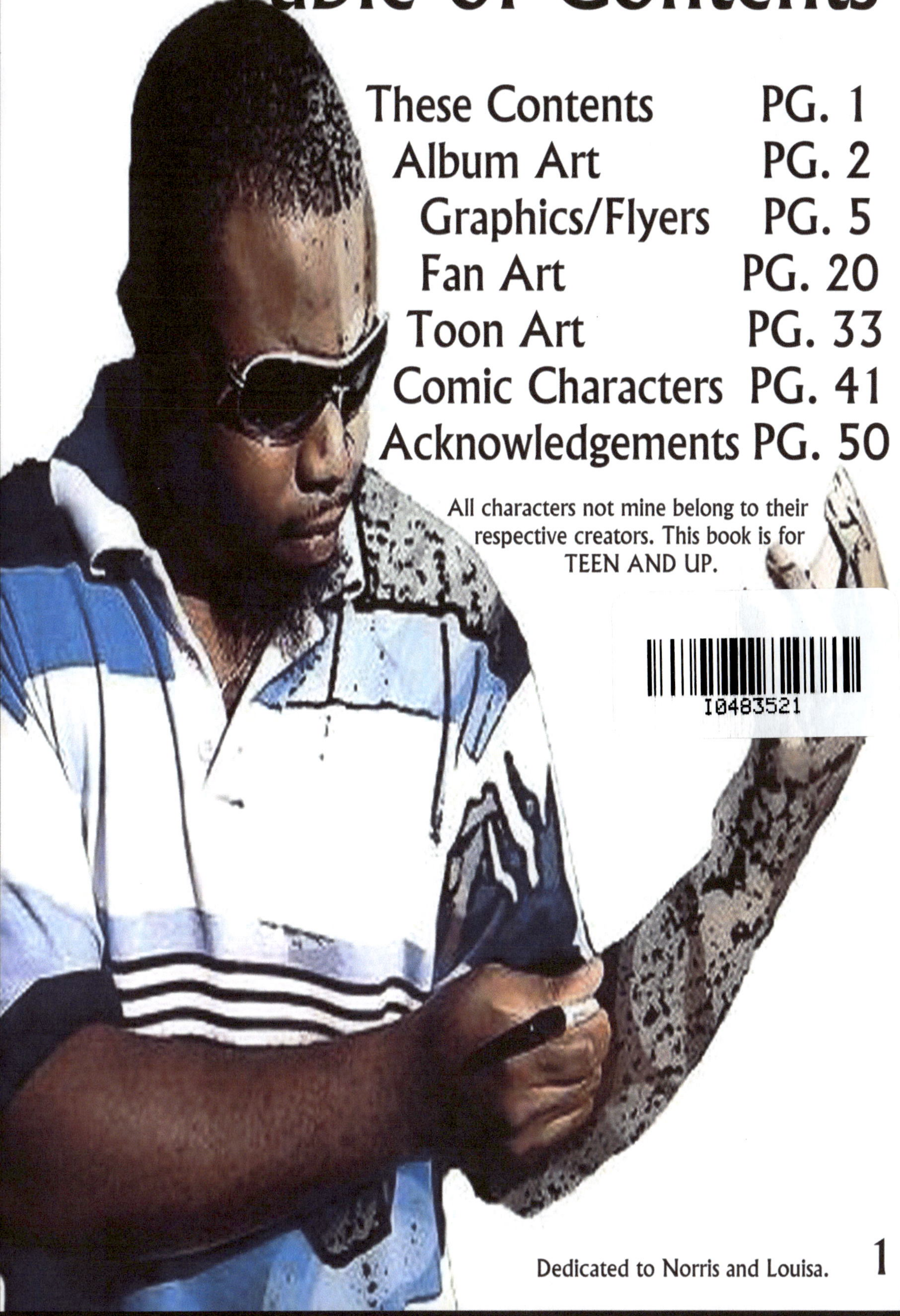

I0483521

Dedicated to Norris and Louisa.

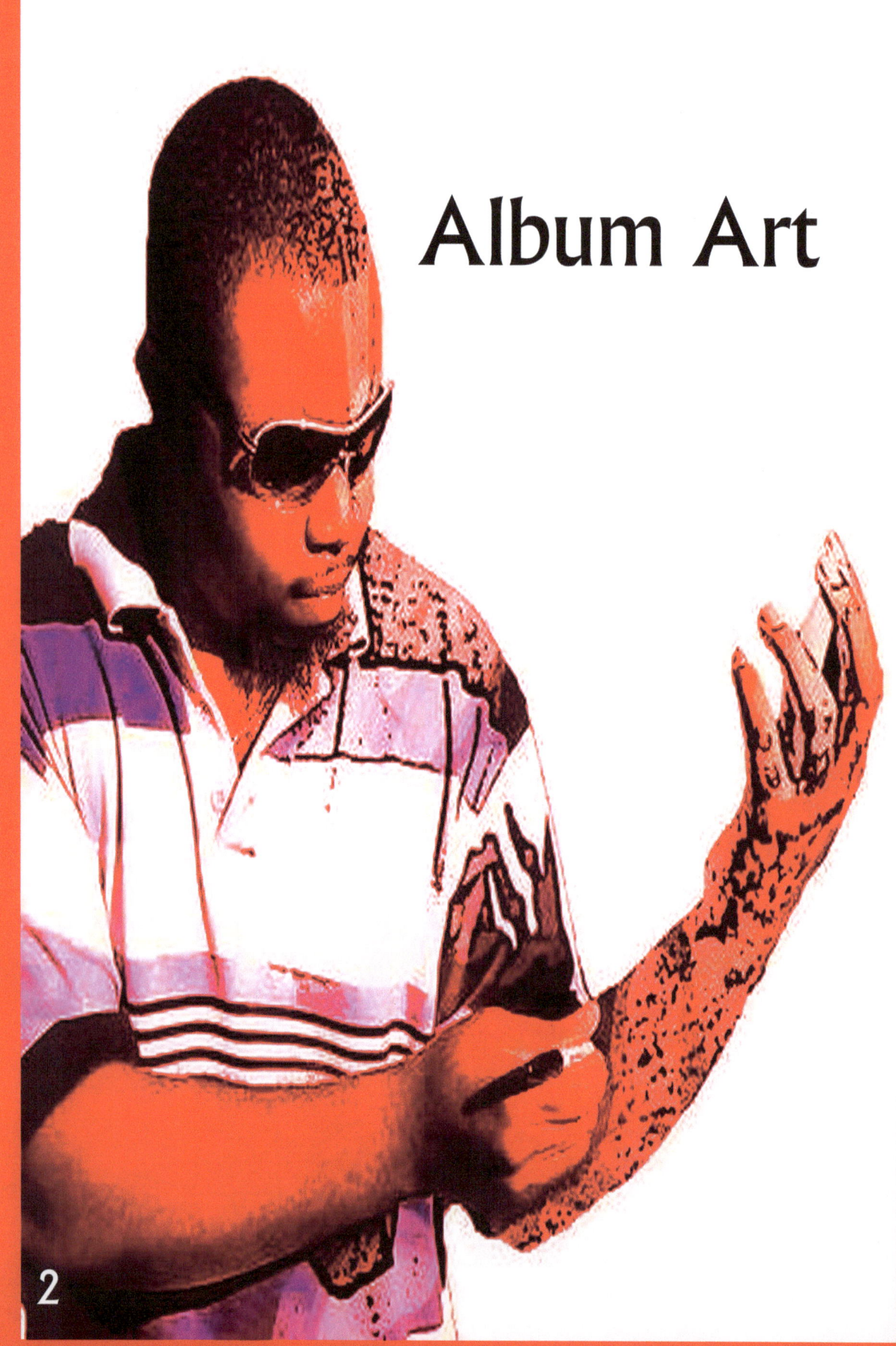

Album Art

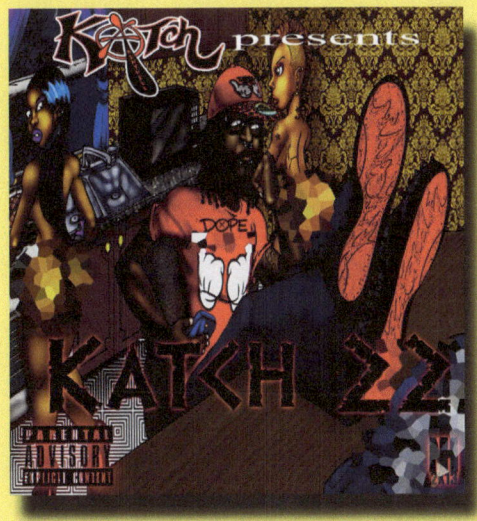

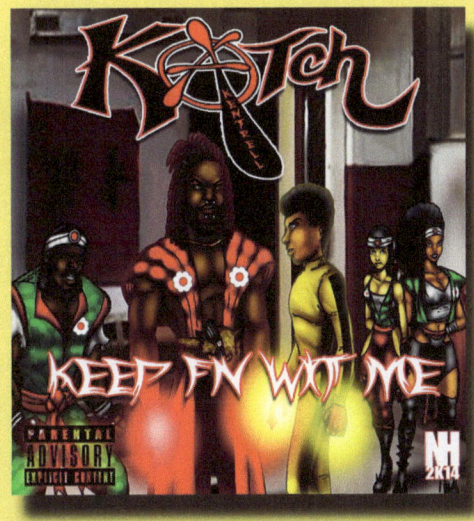

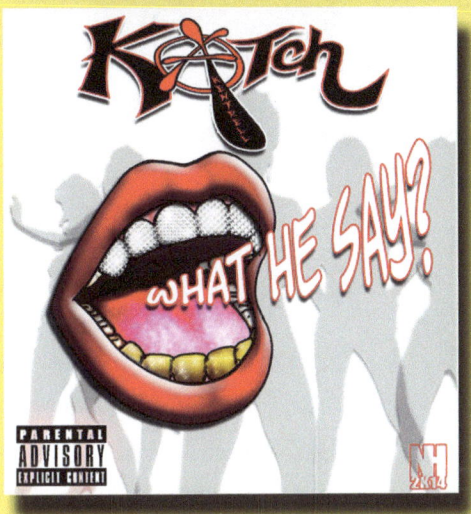

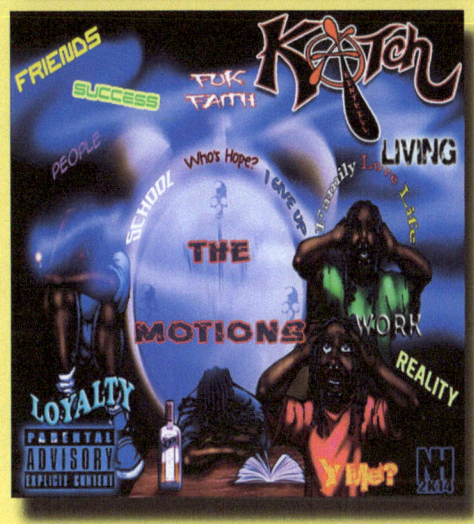

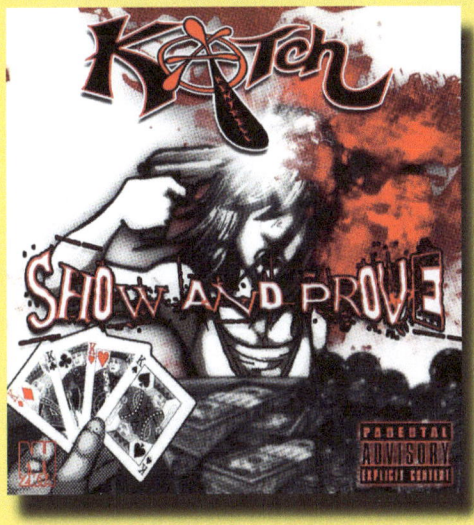

These were single covers (and main album cover) I did for Rap Artist Katch Kentrell. I would say they came out well.

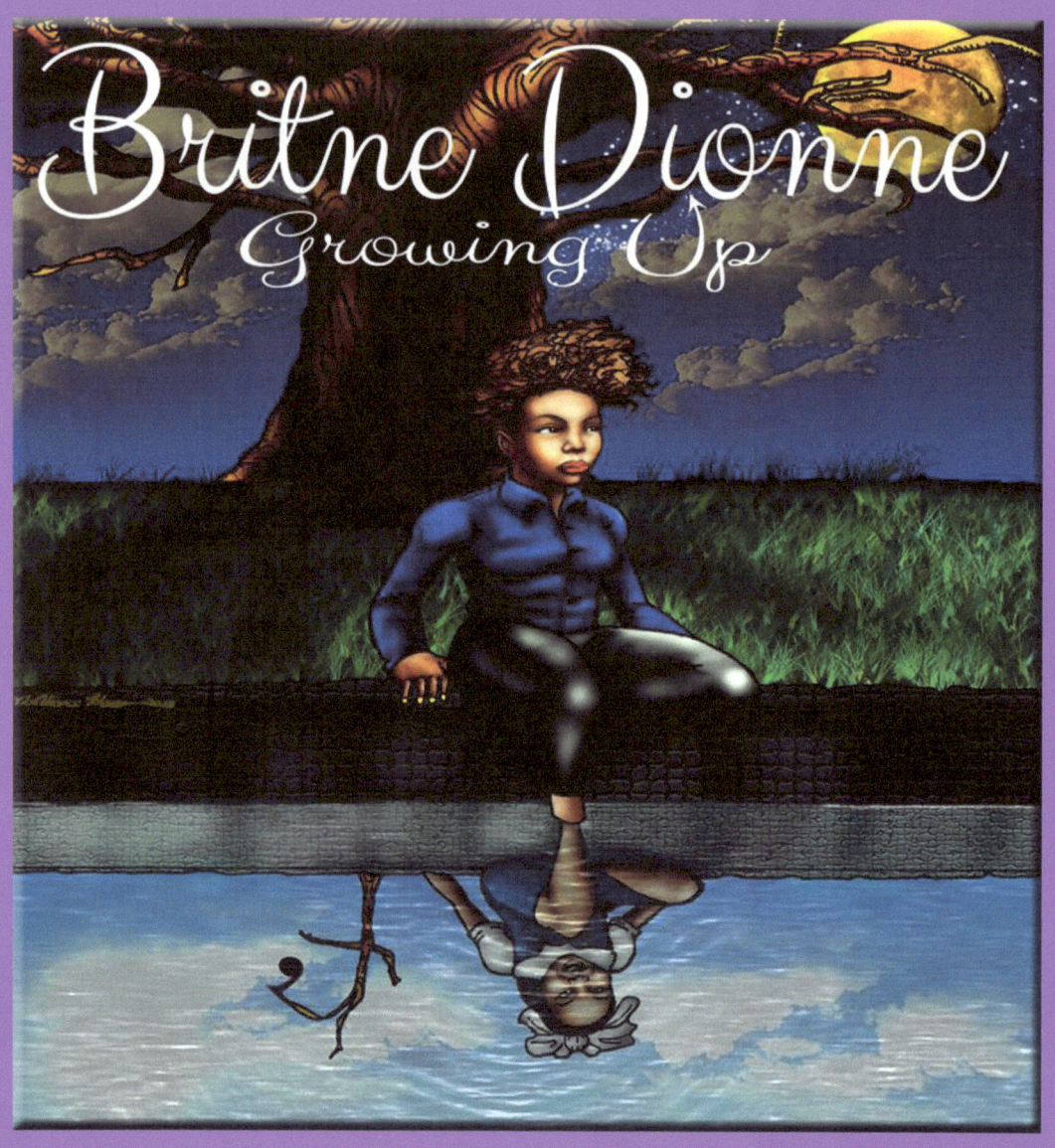

Britne Dionne
Growing Up

Just over three years ago, this young lady performed at my cousin's birthday party/concert aka The Shindig. A dope singer she is, we kept in touch and a few months later I did this cover for her EP. More to come from this talent.

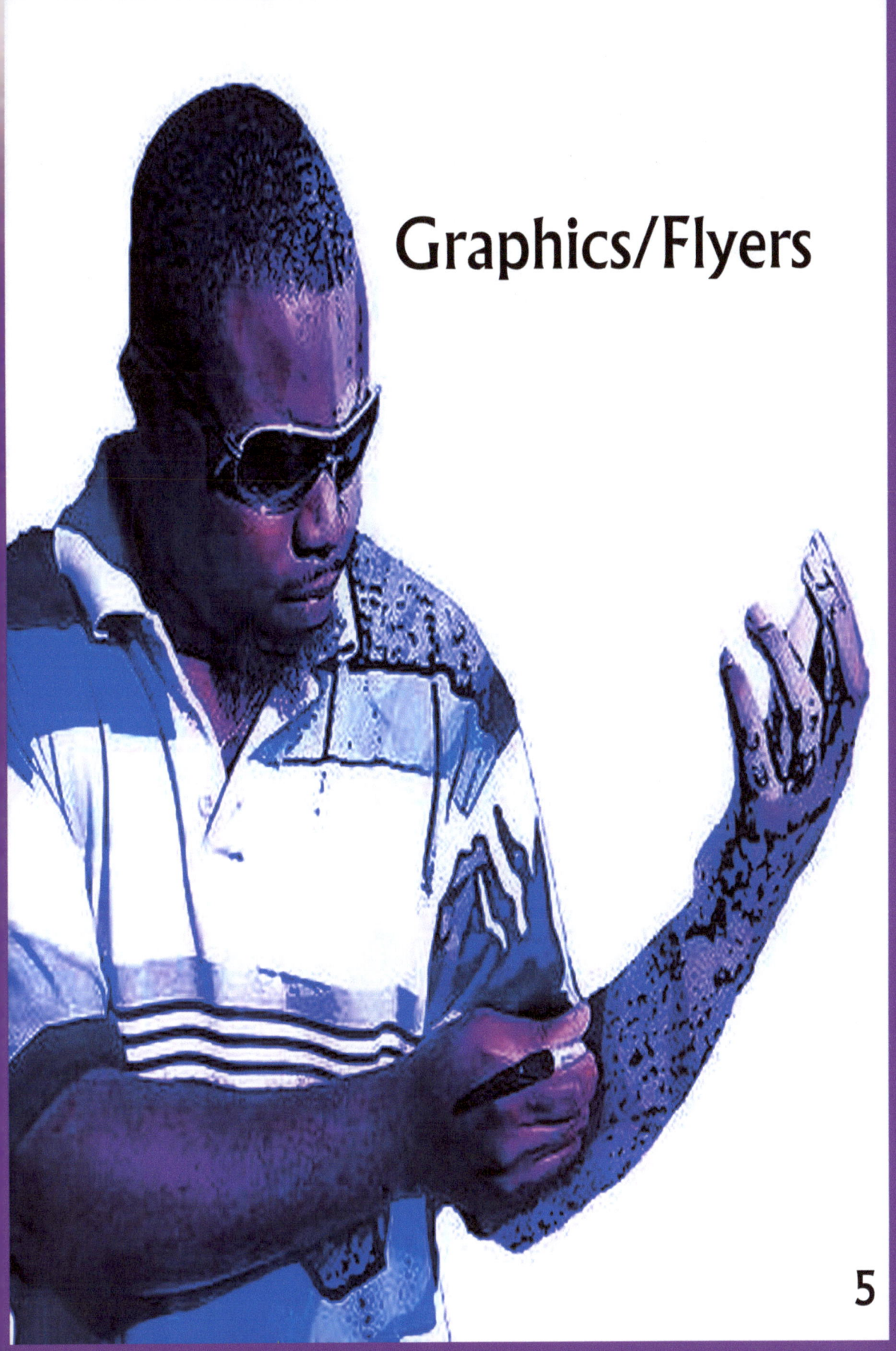

Graphics/Flyers

BRITNE DIONNE

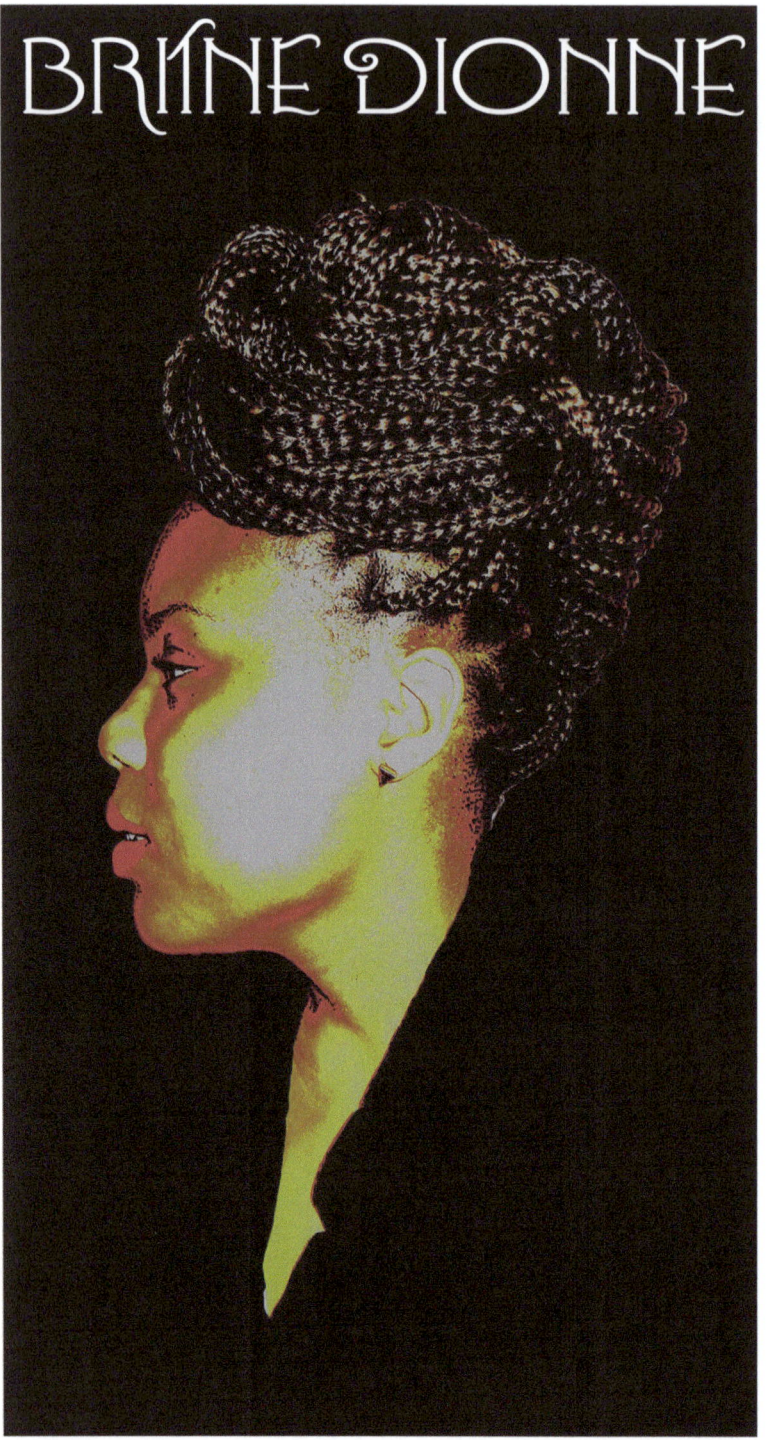

While at the listening party for Britne Dionne's EP *Growing Up*, I took a look at the way she was wearing her braids looking all queen like. So I told her "Hey, turn to the side." I took her pic. She had no idea wth I was doing!! That's usually the case when you're making art. I took the pic and created this. She has been using it ever since. I knew that this shot would be iconic for her.

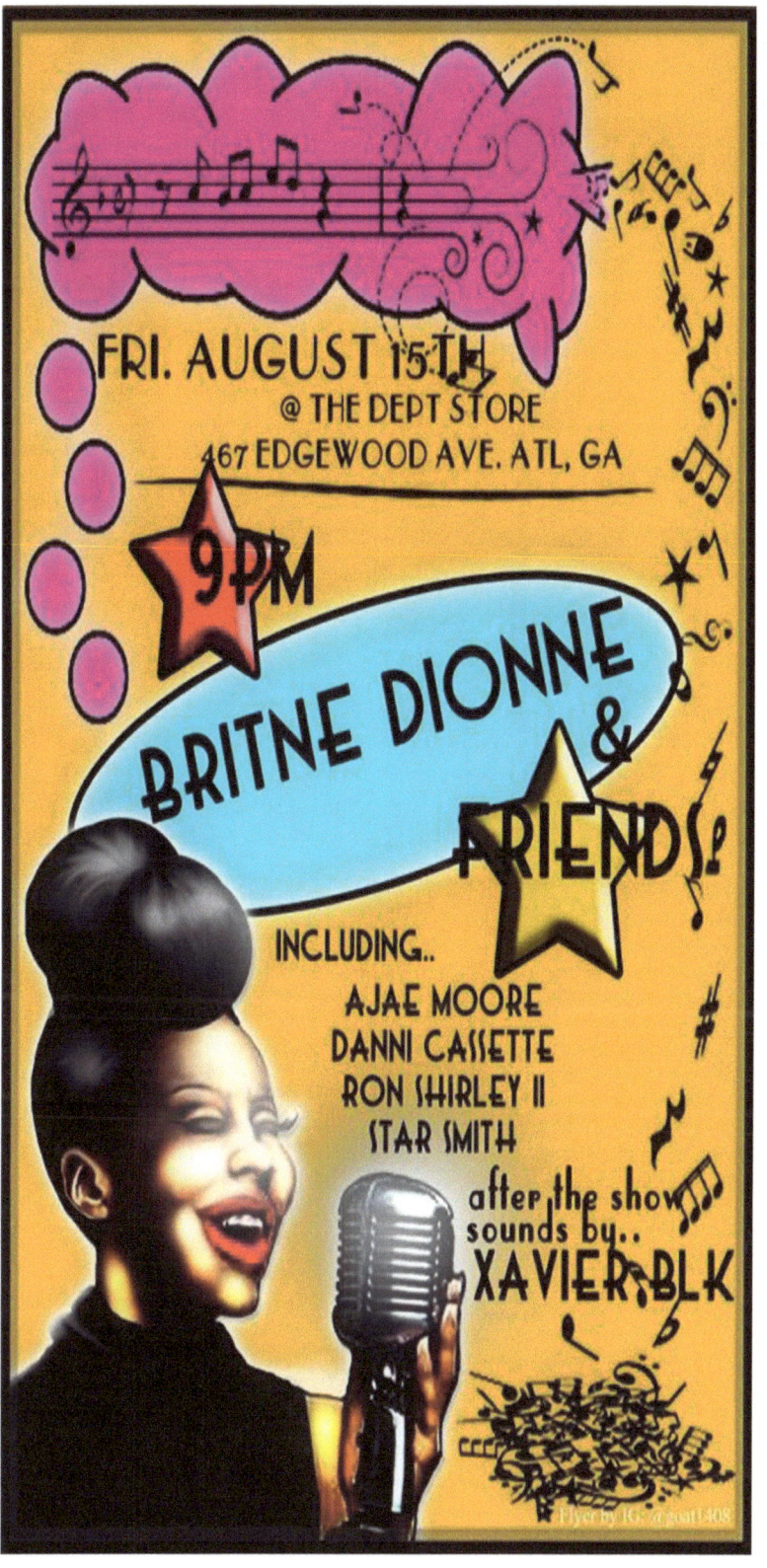

Britne Dionne wanted to get a new drawing of her for her new flyer. We did an awesome collab on bringing this to fruition. She found an Ella Fitzgerald flyer and we spruced it up. I placed her art double, colored the flyer and BD did the text. It came out great. She would go on to use her art twin on several more flyers throughout the next year or two.

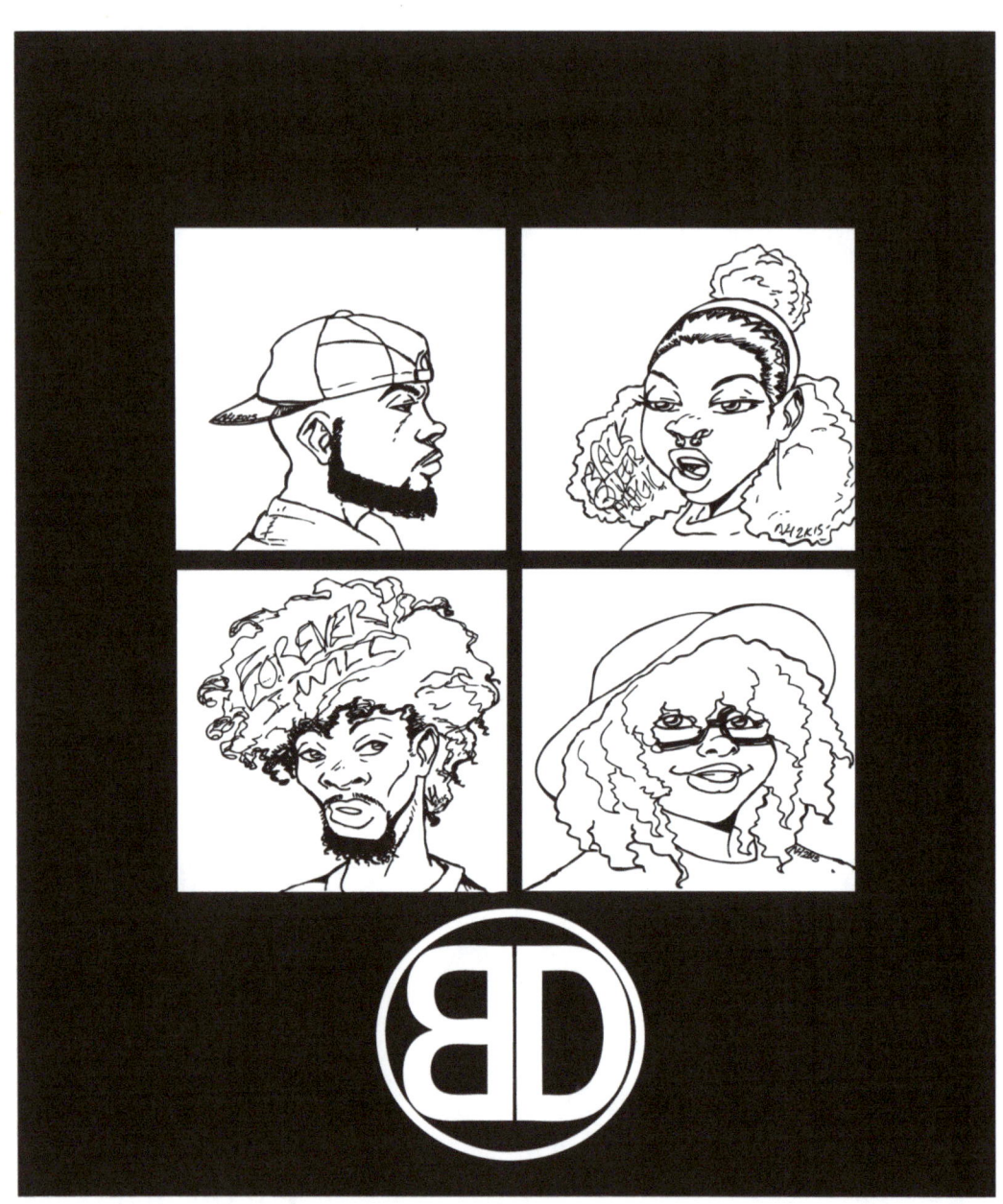

In 2015, Britne Dionne began her Rooftop Riot shows. She tagged me on board to do the flyer for the events. Here is the original linework for the first flyer.

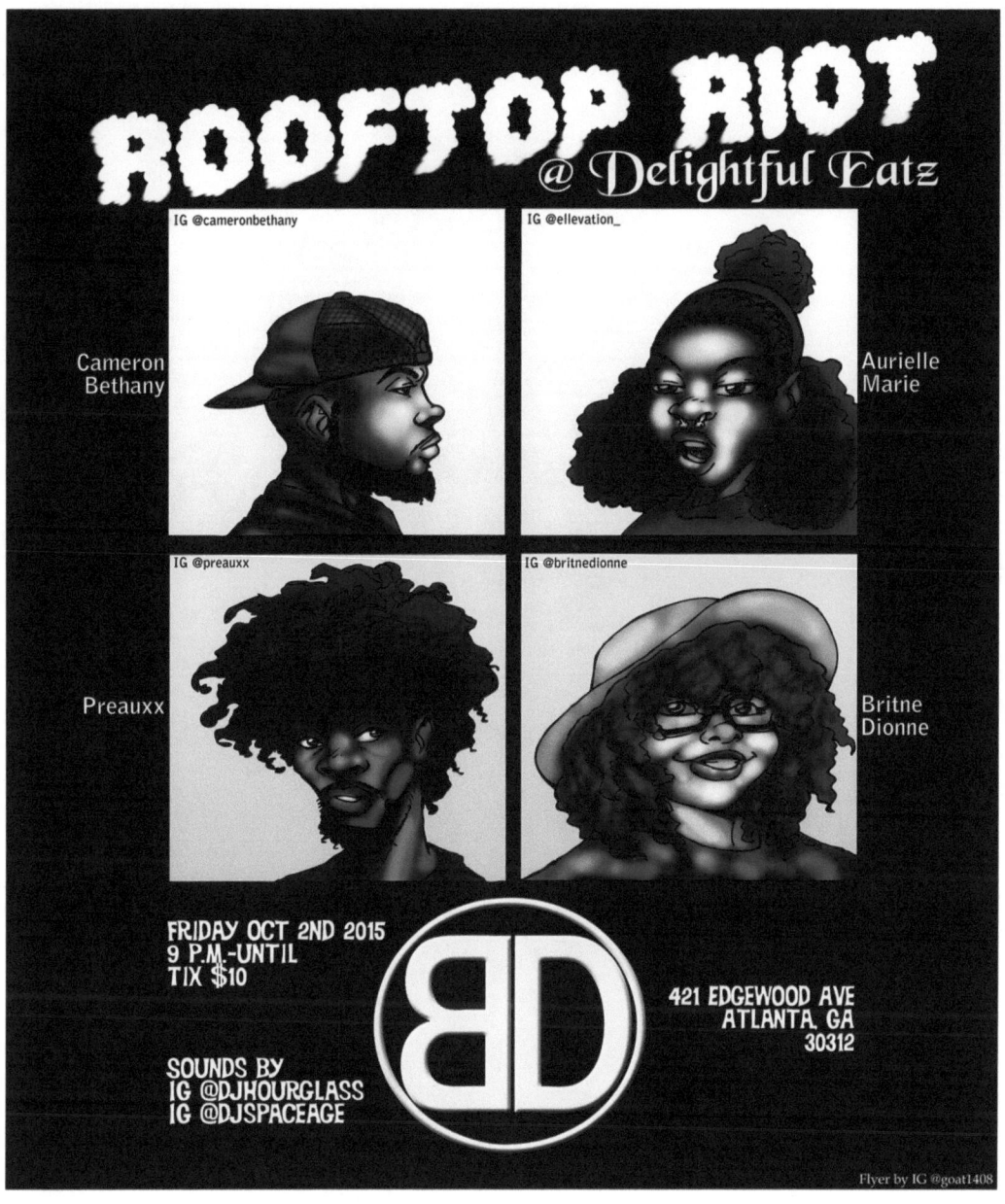

The final version of the first Rooftop Riot flyer. It came out pretty dope. Shoutouts to all of these dope performers...they are good!! If you know me and my taste in music you know that is legit.

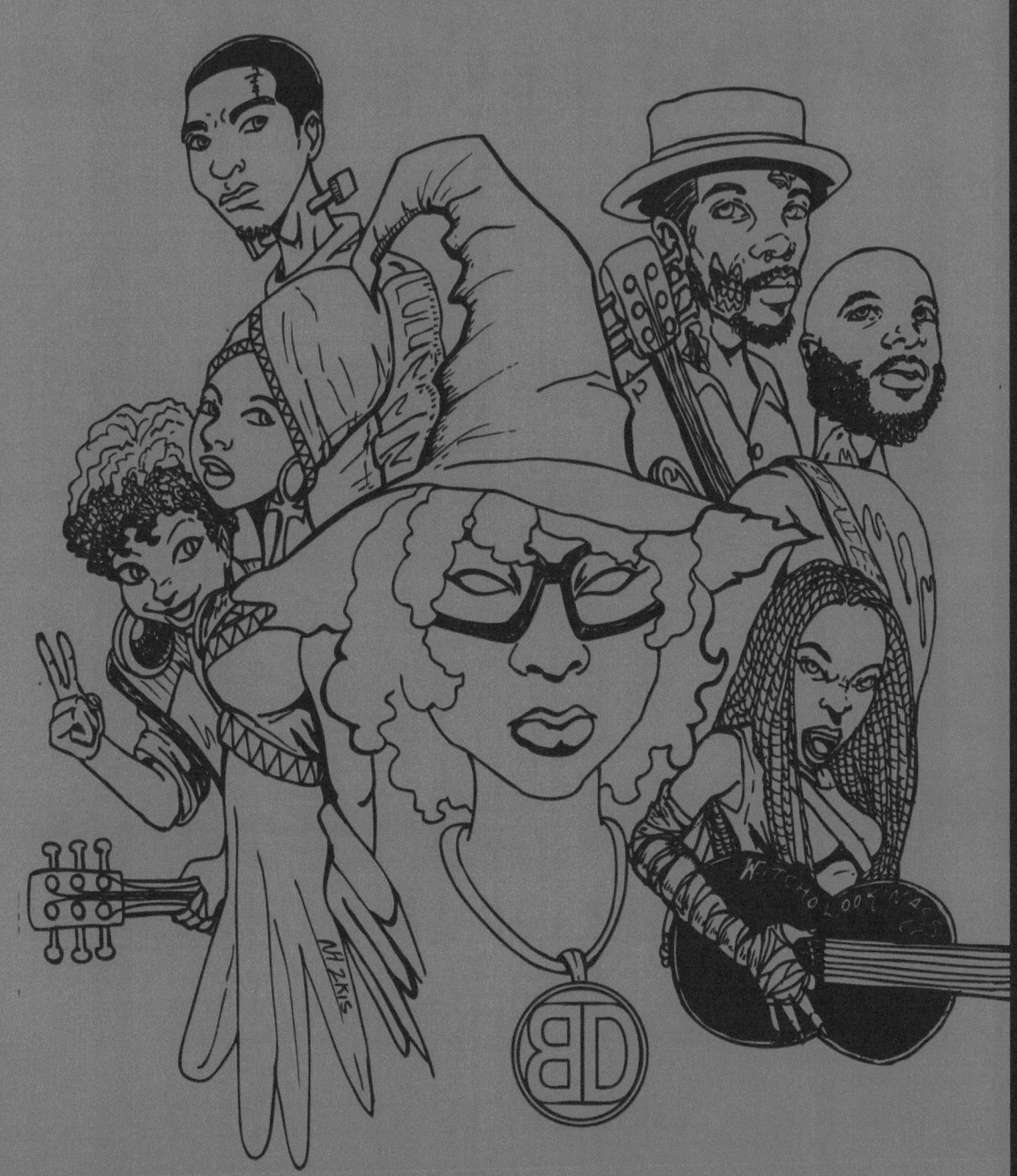

For the 2nd Rooftop Riot, which took place on Halloween, appropriate measures was taken. I enjoyed doing this piece :)

Here's the final version (without text). Shoutouts to these amazing artists and DJs who performed there, kudos to (clockwise L-R) my folk Guitar Gabby (in white and yellow), DJ Hourglass (Thriller jacket), DJ Nah Mean (bolts in neck), DJ Jay Marz (zombie), Daiyaan (with blood on neck) and Melody Reyne (with guitar).

This book in your hands is fresh! How fresh? Some of the art in this book (as I write this) isn't even a month old!!! As of matter of fact, as I type this I'm thinking of a piece that I'm going to add to the Toon Art section!! I'll talk more about them when you flip over to those pages, lol. Now, this flyer for Britne Dionne was for her event that took place just fifteen days ago in my time, Valentine's Day 2016. Britne and these other four talents did their renditions of songs from the classic 2003 album *The Love Below*, by Andre 3000 of OutKast.

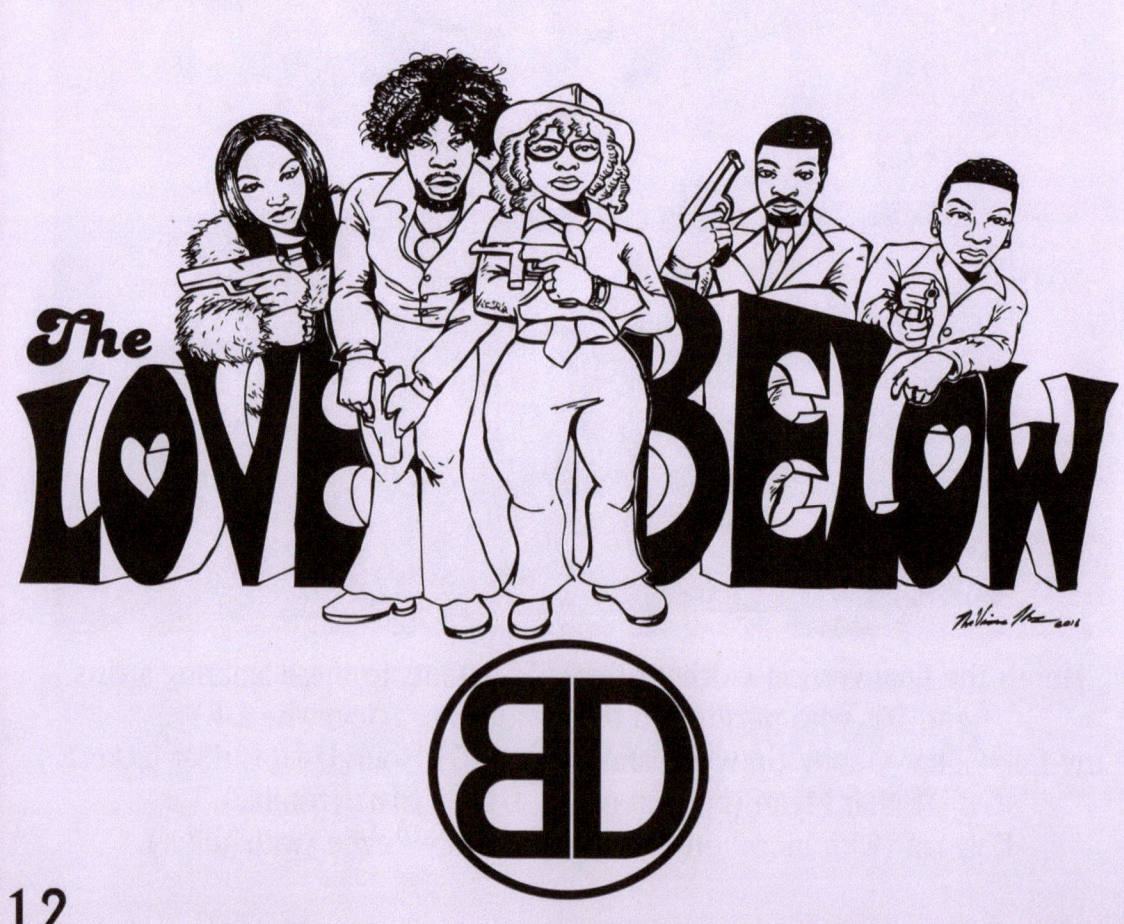

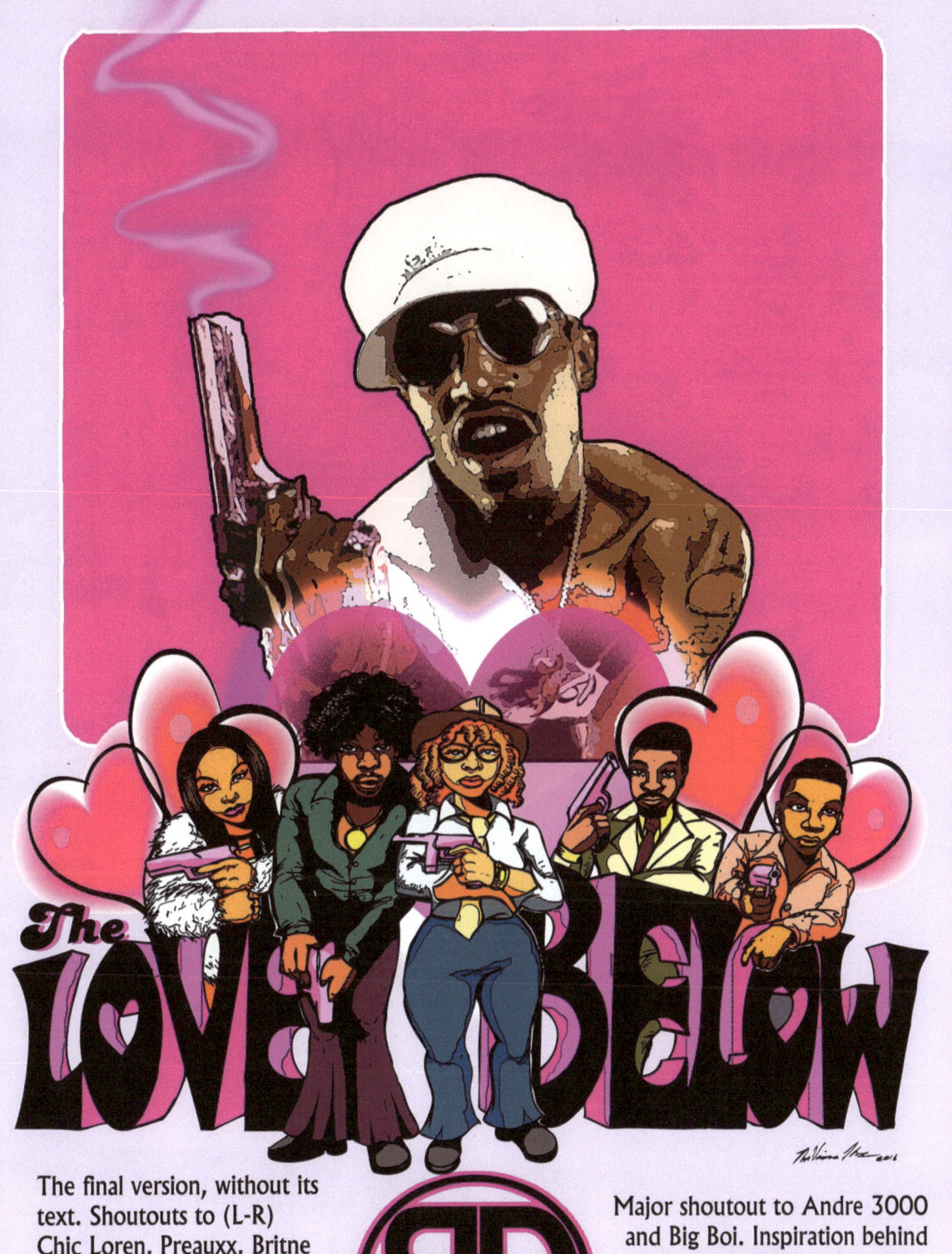

THE LOVE BELOW

The final version, without its text. Shoutouts to (L-R) Chic Loren, Preauxx, Britne Dionne, Ron Shirley II and Danni Cassette for a dope show. Flyer paid homage to the movie poster for *Black Caesar*. Hey BD, tell Janelle Monae to holla at me :) Fan since 2006 :)

Major shoutout to Andre 3000 and Big Boi. Inspiration behind the name Slim Jim Longfoot. The South STILL got something to say.

13

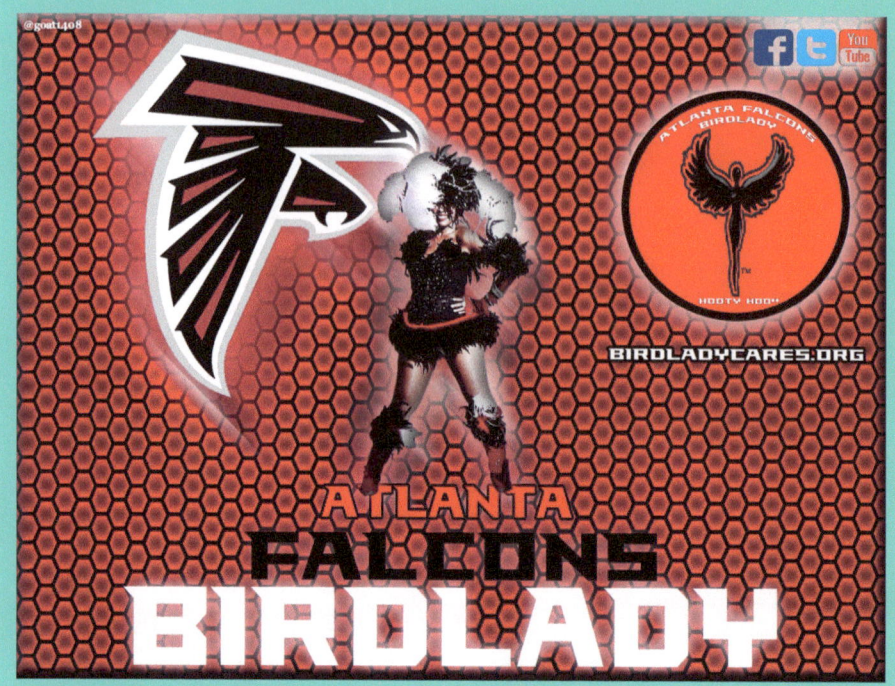

Graphic I did for Carolyn "AF Birdlady" Freeman

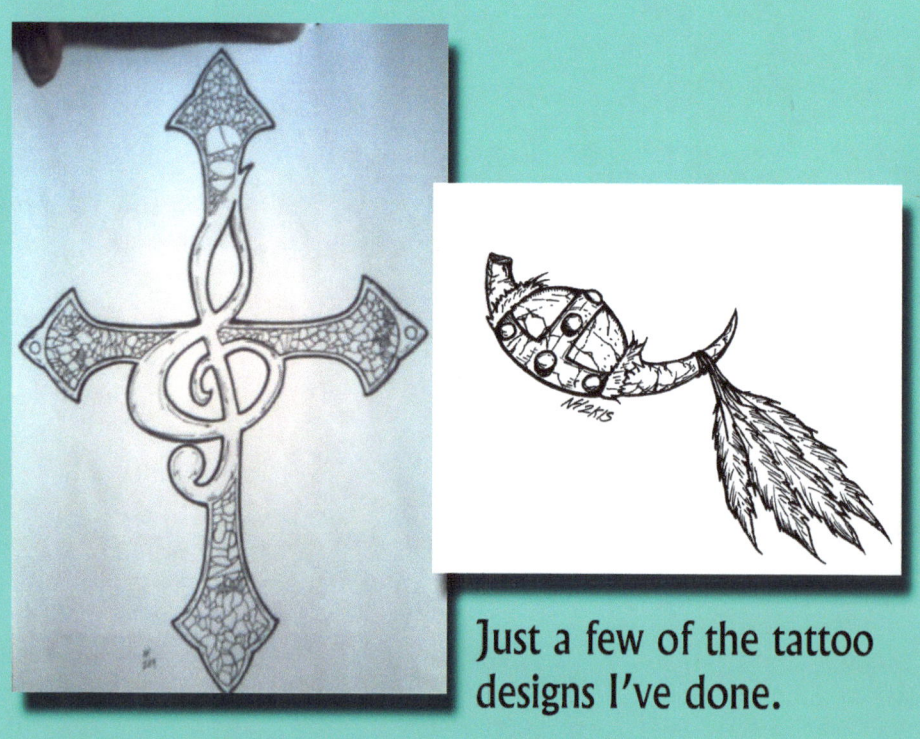

Just a few of the tattoo
designs I've done.

Flyer I did for the single *We In Atlanta* by Tanneh & The Godz. Tanneh Snohti is the artist who introduced me to her friend singer Britne Dionne. These young ladies are dope with their music. Rightfully so with Tanneh, she is my lil' cuz. :)

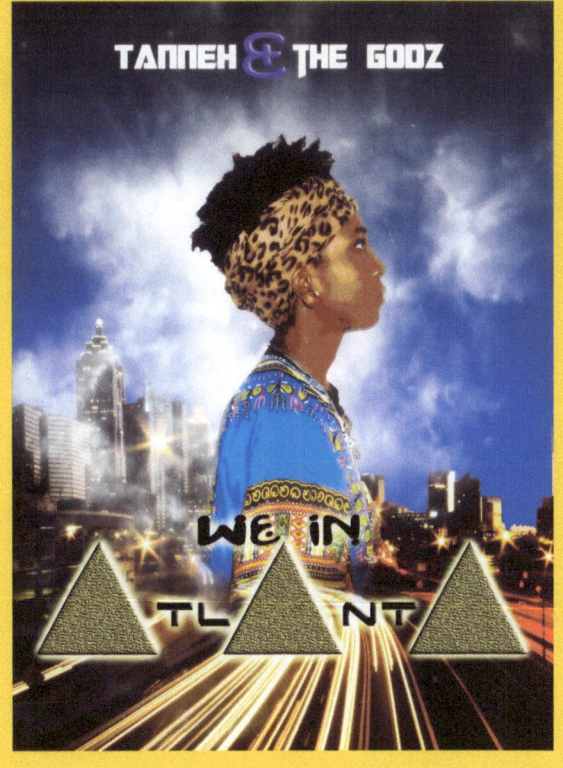

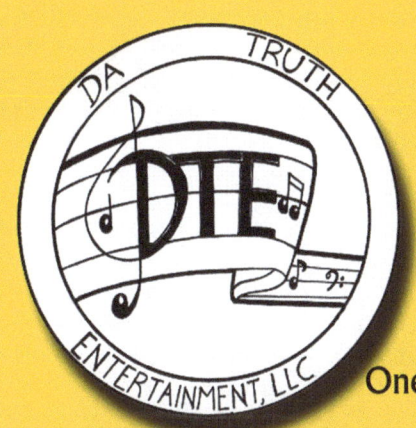

One of many business logos I've done.

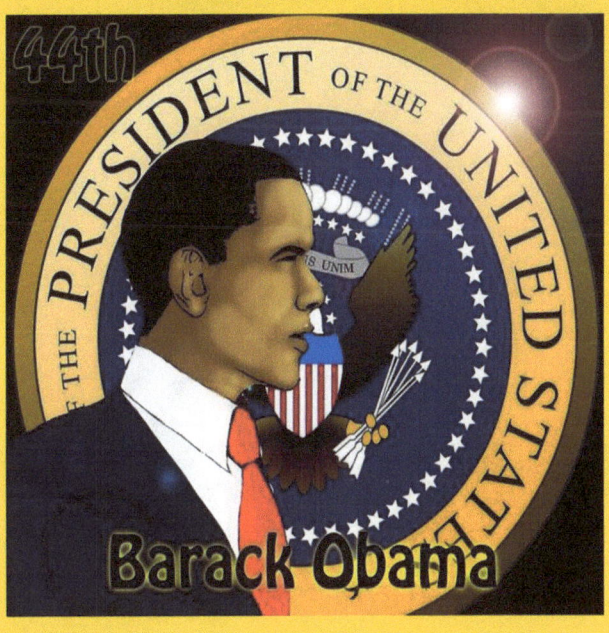

I did this piece the day after Barack H. Obama became the 44th U.S. President. With this being his last full calendar year in office I figure it would be fitting to put in here for future generations. His 2nd term is a blur to me. Election Day 2012 I lost my mom.

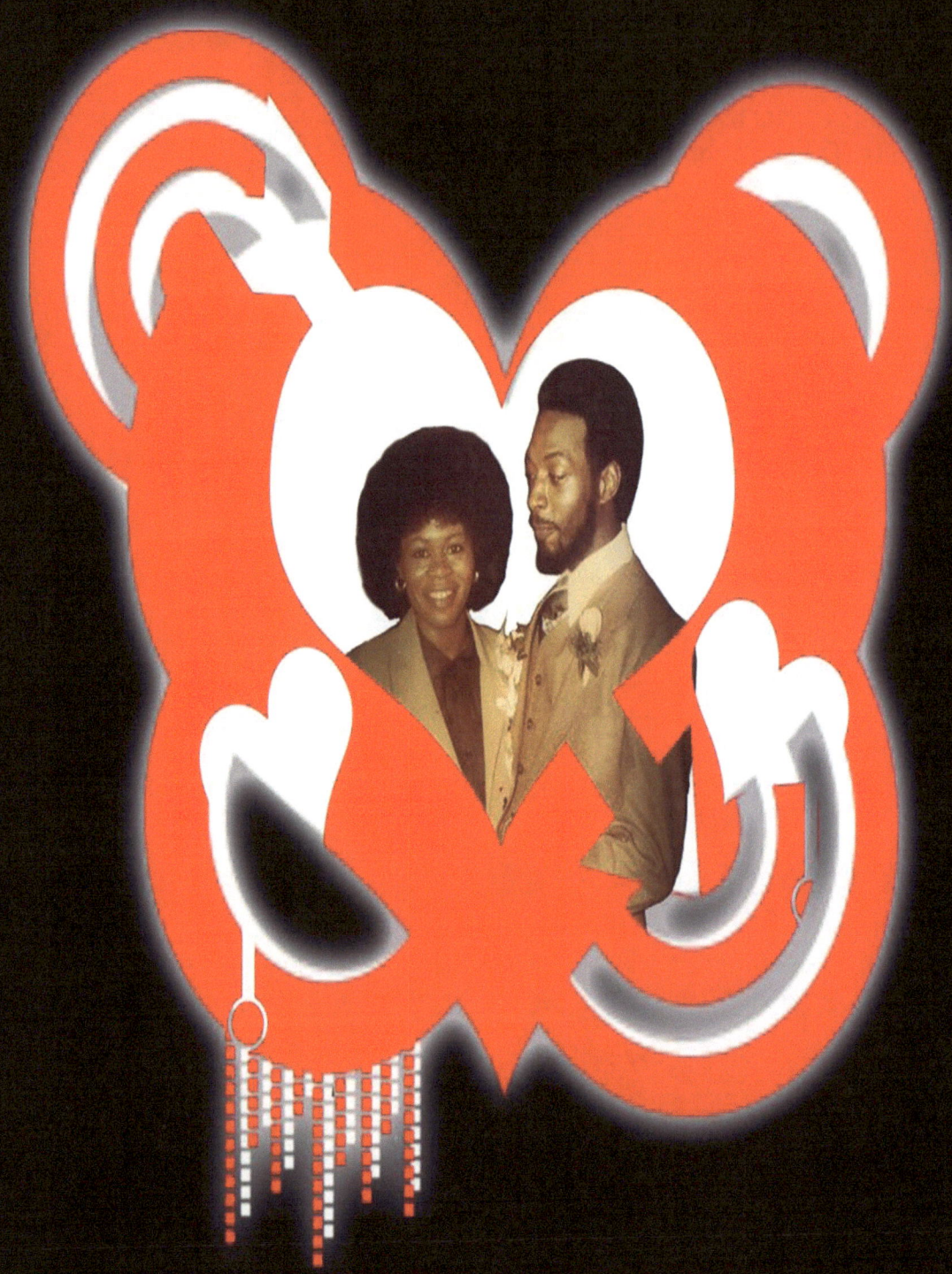

Thankful and blessed that I had/have
these two in my life.

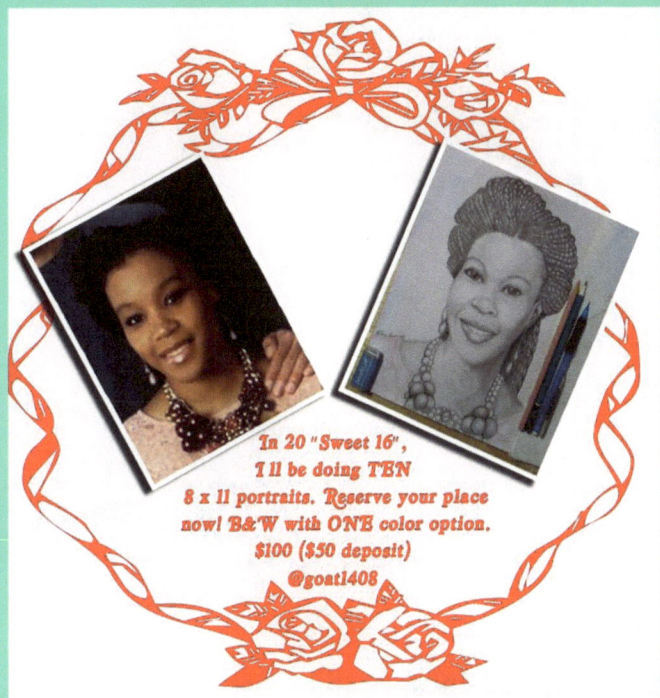

If you're reading this and it's still 2016, You should definitely jump on this. At this present time I still have all ten spots open!

In 20 "Sweet 16",
I'll be doing TEN
8 x 11 portraits. Reserve your place now! B&W with ONE color option.
$100 ($50 deposit)
@goat1408

The IndyCon idea began in the summer of 2015. The first IndyCon was held Oct. 10-11th. Now at present time we are in full swing of kicking off IndyCon 2! Hope to see you there and at all the ones to possibly come!! Visit the website

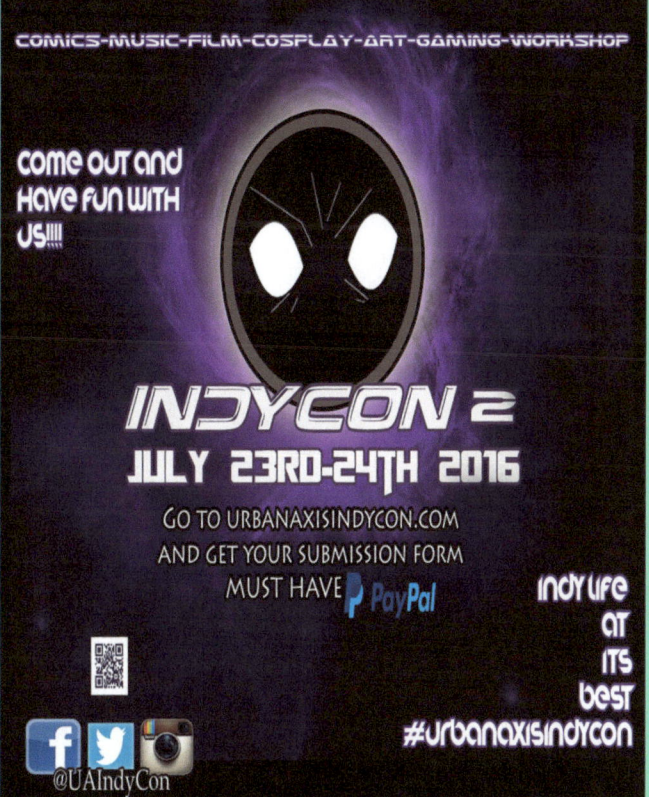

COMICS-MUSIC-FILM-COSPLAY-ART-GAMING-WORKSHOP

COME OUT AND HAVE FUN WITH US!!!!

INDYCON 2
JULY 23RD-24TH 2016

GO TO URBANAXISINDYCON.COM
AND GET YOUR SUBMISSION FORM
MUST HAVE PayPal

INDY LIFE
AT
ITS
BEST
#urbanaxisindycon

@UAIndyCon

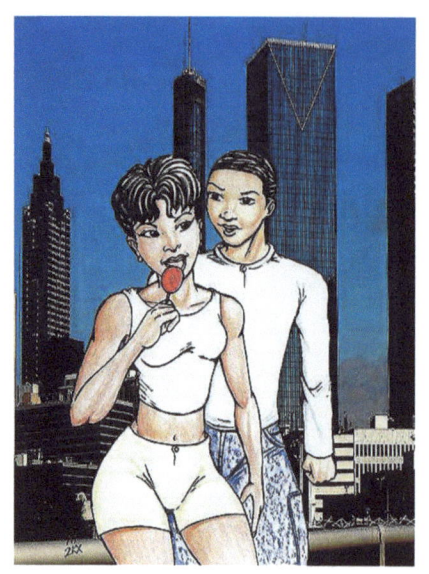 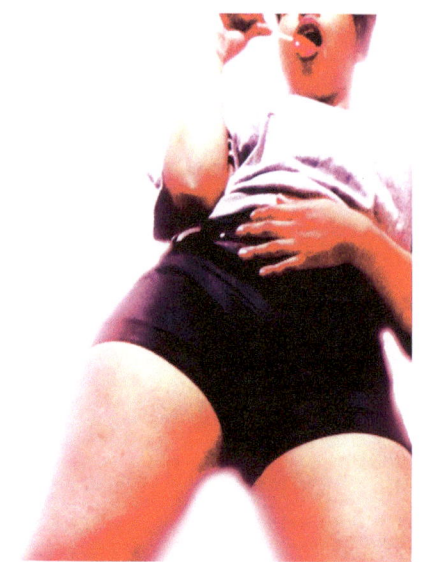

Art from the original cover of the urban
book *Getting some Pookie* and the new cover
for *Getting some Pookie The Remix*. Model's name
is listed in the Acknowledgements of *Getting
some Pookie The Remix*, out NOW!!

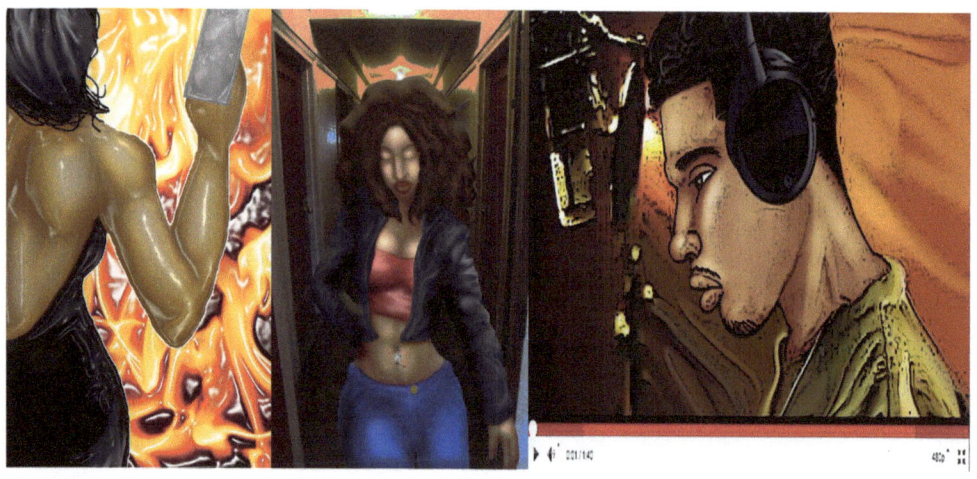

Art from the first three volumes of *Hotter than fire, wetter than water*.
The sequel series of *Getting some Pookie*. Volumes 1 & 2 available now!!!
Volume 3 is coming soon.......MATURE READERS ONLY

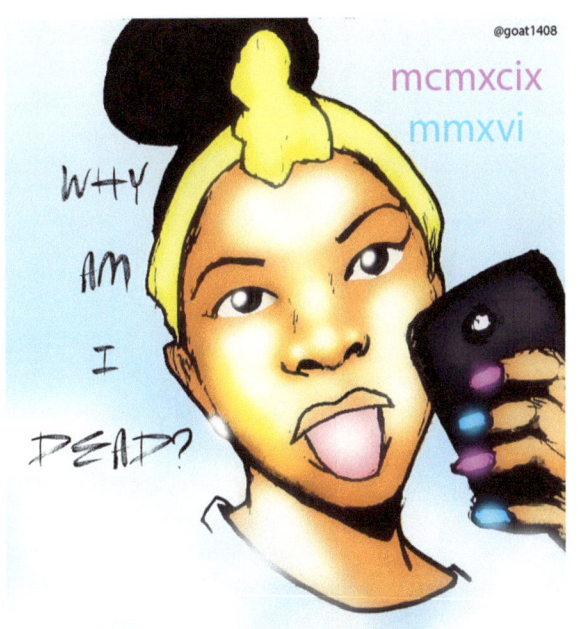

This girl was MURDERED!! Point blank. Rest in peace Gynnya.......

#JusticeForGynnya

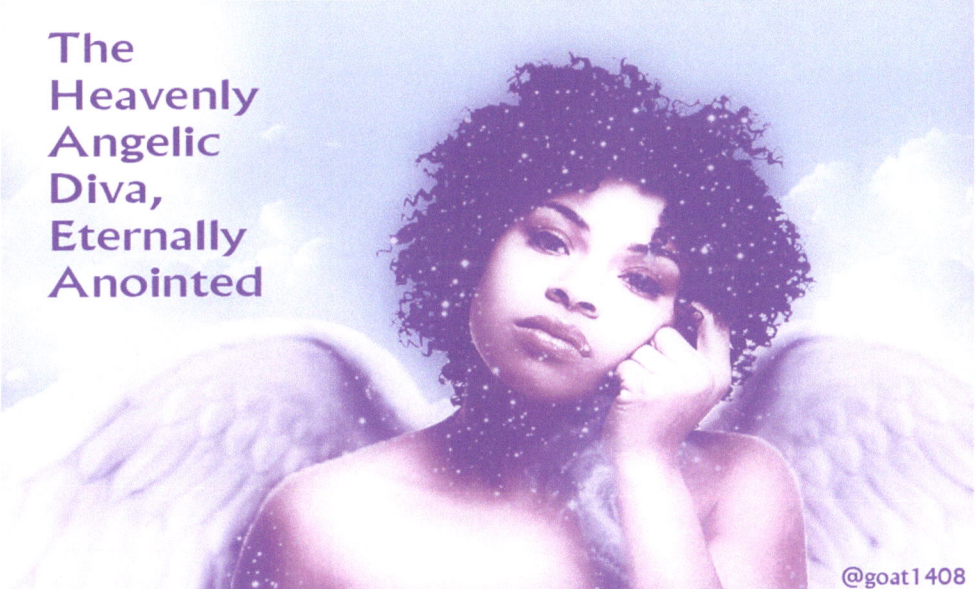

The Heavenly Angelic Diva, Eternally Anointed

@goat1408

As I type this, I must tell you all something. I am from the future, like beyond the guy who wrote the acknowledgements. You'll understand what I mean by page 39 and 40. I have spent the entire week from Leap Day until today (Mar. 4th) editing this book and working on a margin problem up until earlier today. Then, I found out about this. My friend Thadea Williams was killed in a car accident the early morning of February 28th. This hurts....all you have to do is know her and her light, her love and life was unmistakable. I did this graphic a few hours ago, and I knew I had to put it in this book. Farewell anointed angel. See you next lifetime.

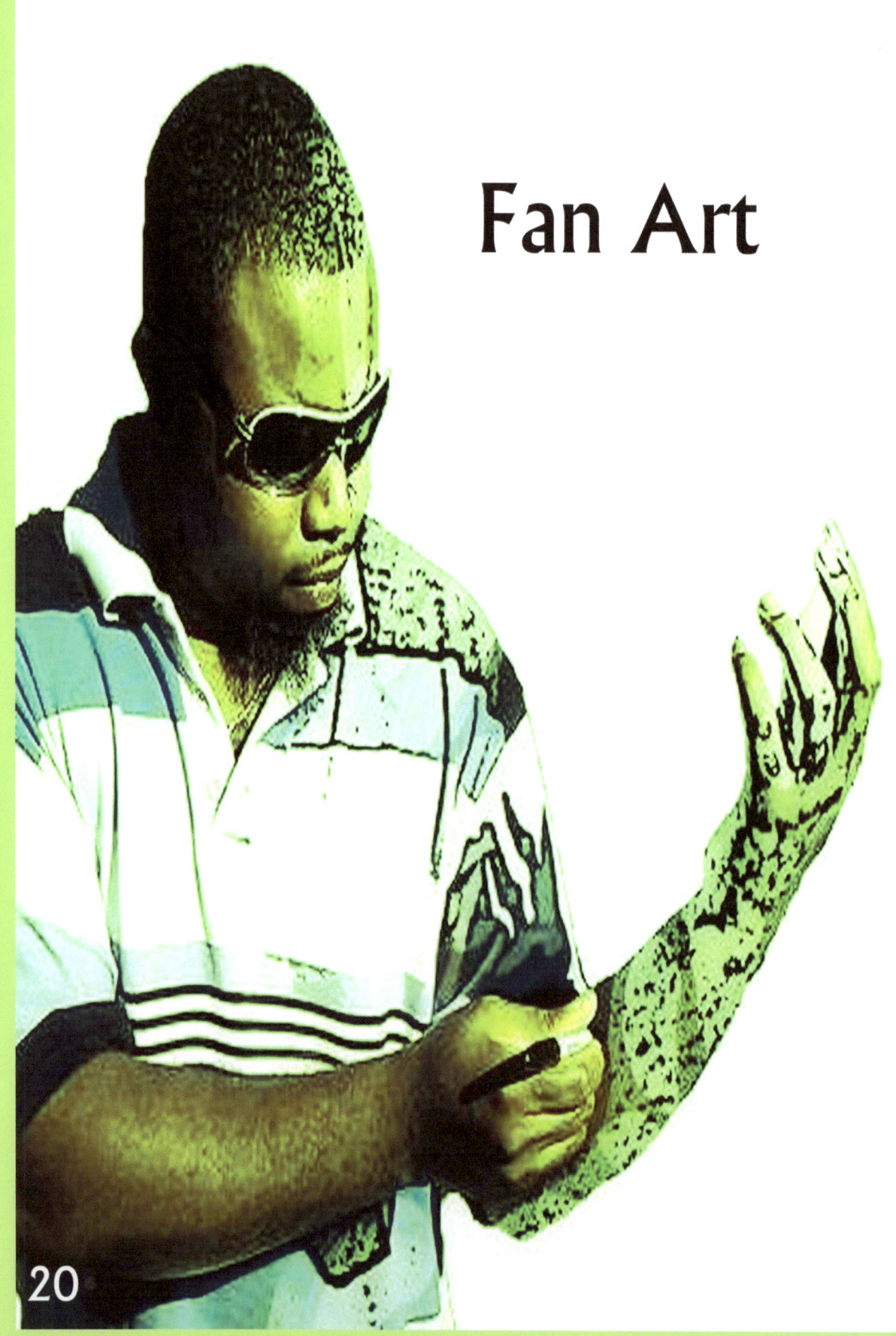

Fan Art

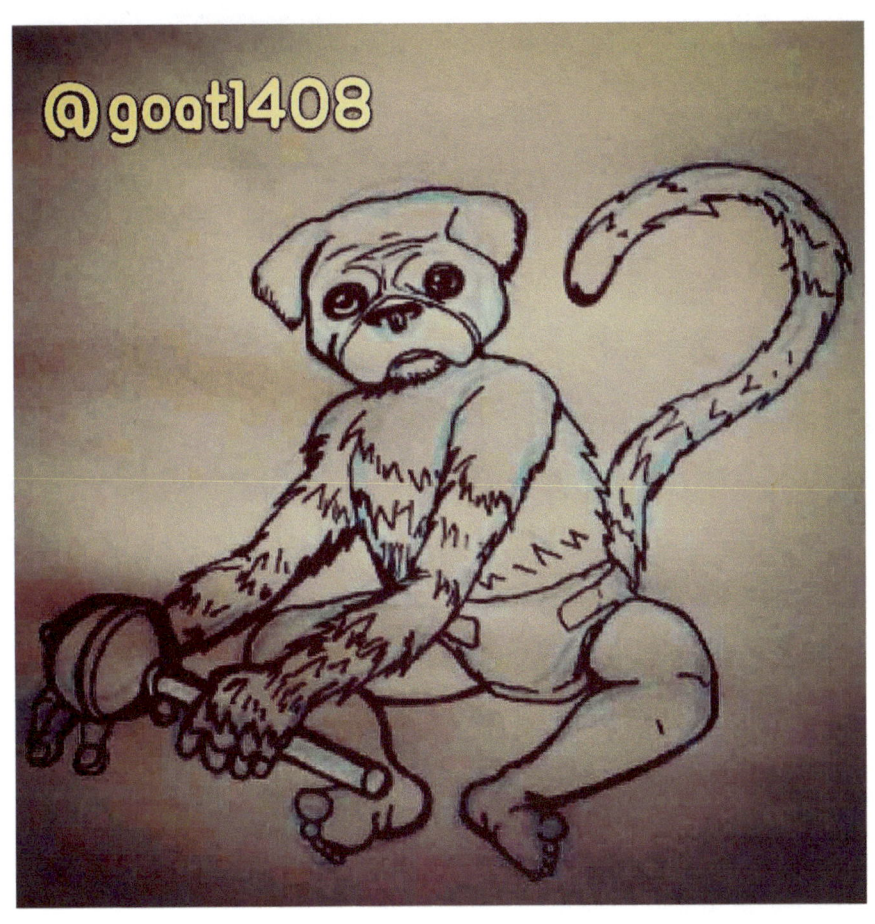

@goat1408

This section showcases Fan Art, in the sense of it all.
Stuff that I like and love.
I would have included art I did of other indy creators'
characters, but I would've had to ask for permission to post them.
For those that don't know, I released this book Beyoncé style....
with no advertising ahead of it. Only person (as I type)
that knows about this book is my dad. I hope that you (the reader)
enjoy this, and my puppymonkeybaby :)

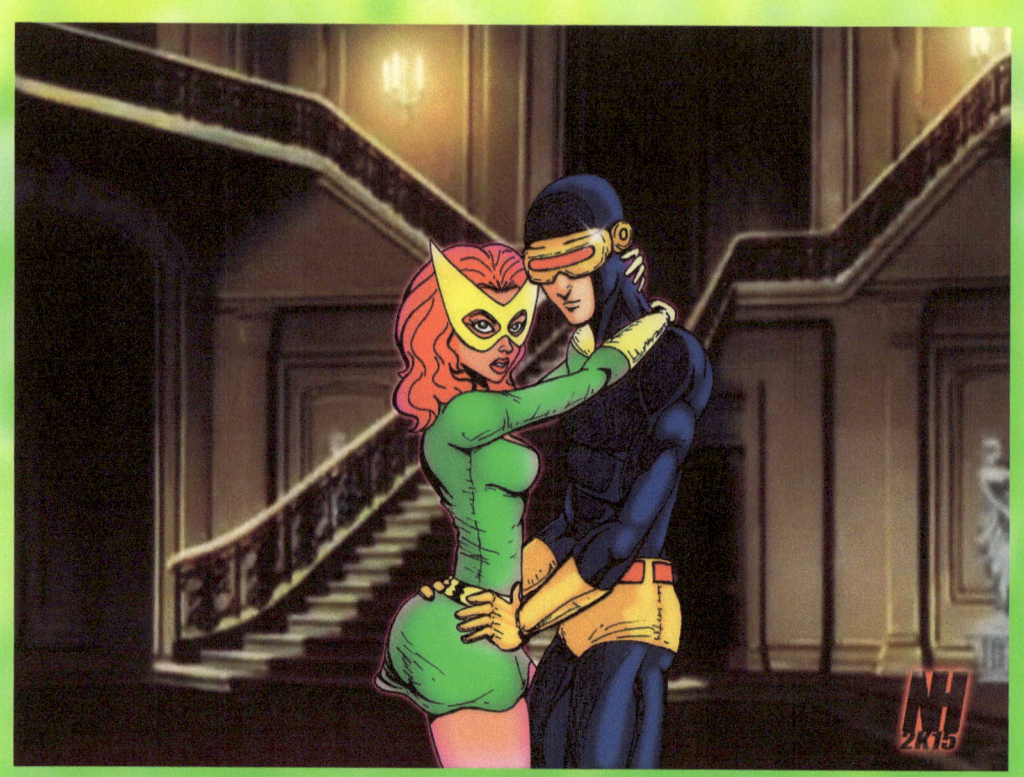

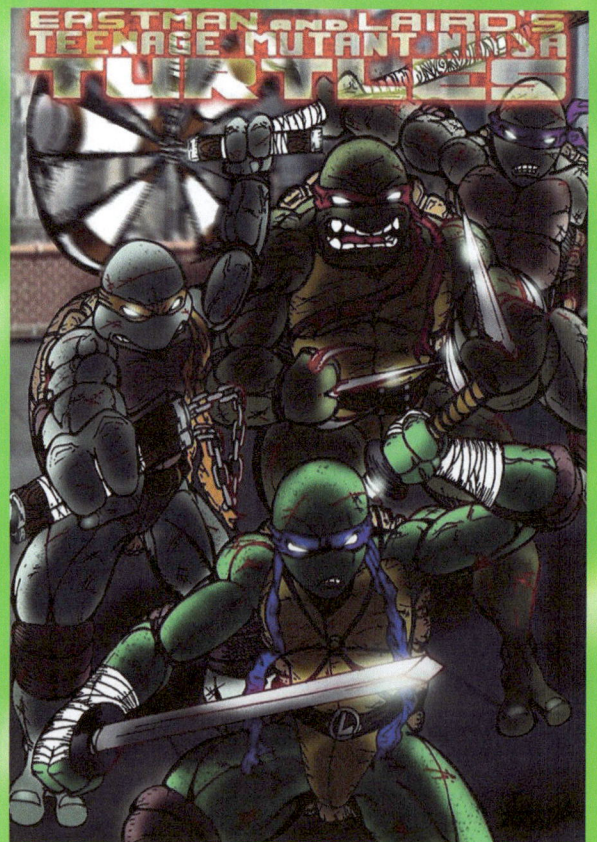

From merry mutants
and mutant ninjas....

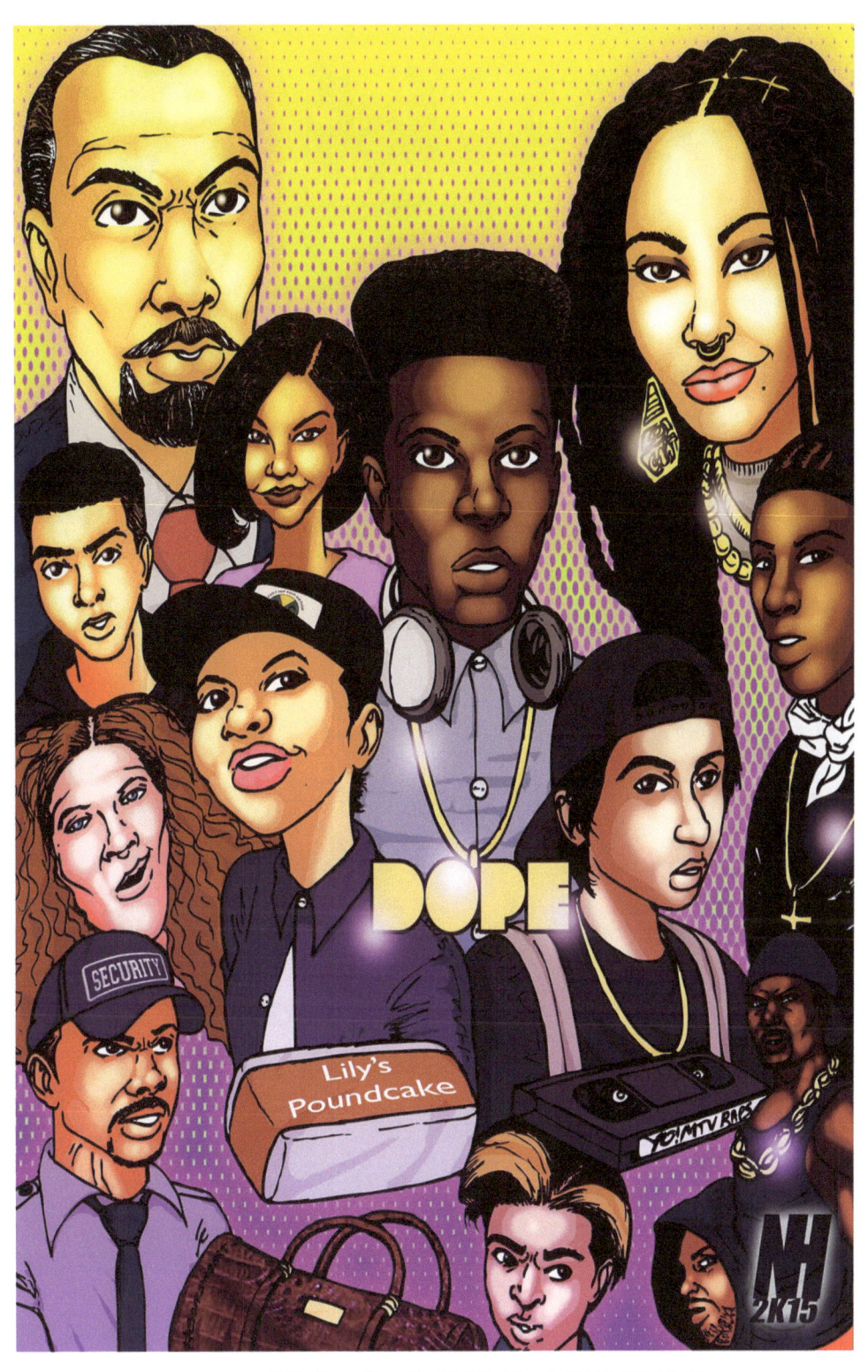

.......TO DOPE MOVIES

The next few pages are from my Smurf Life series I started in 2014. If interest picks back up, I will introduce them as apparel on my site, society6.com/goat1408

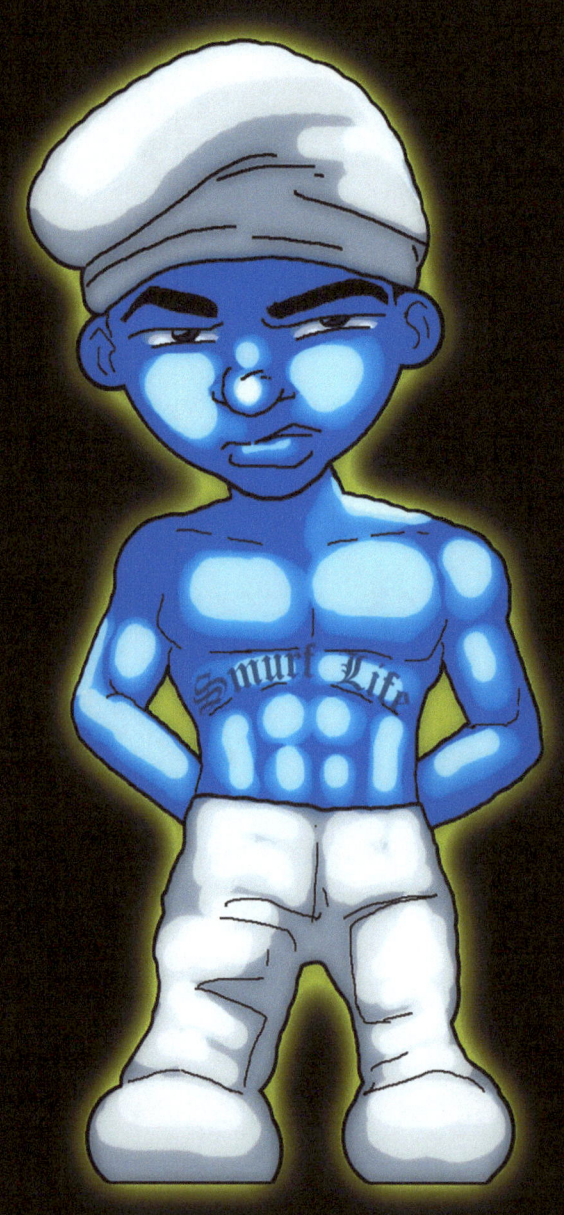

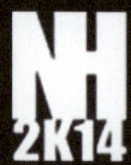

24

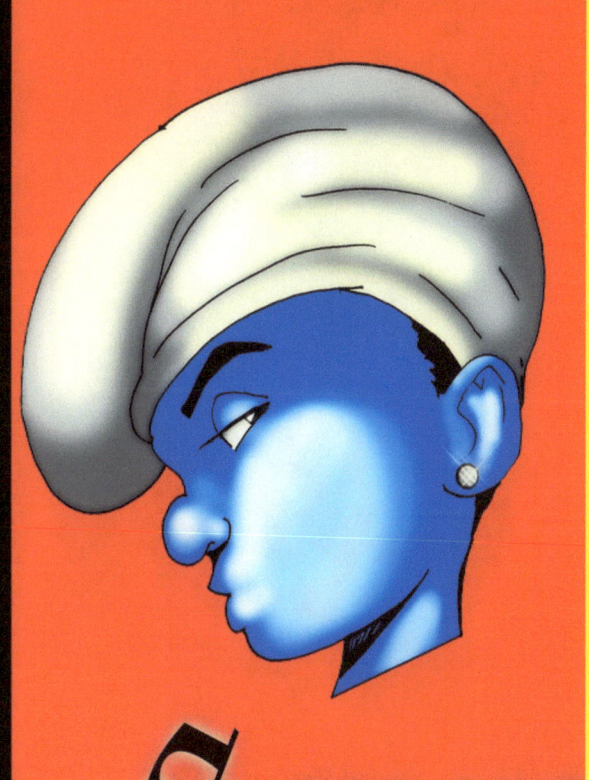
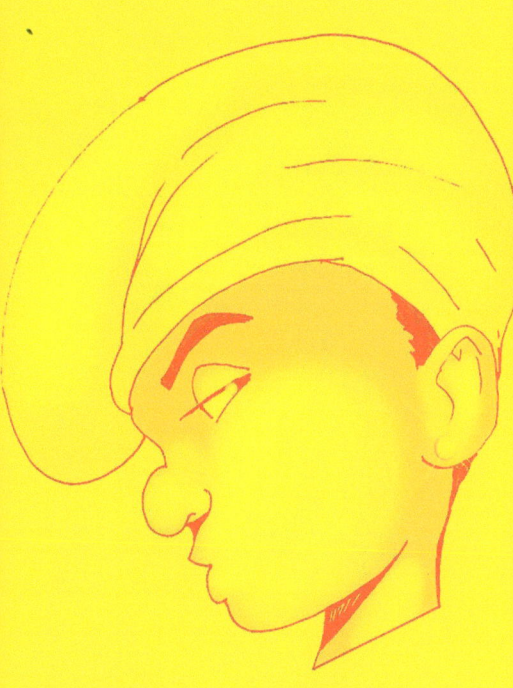

SmurfLife

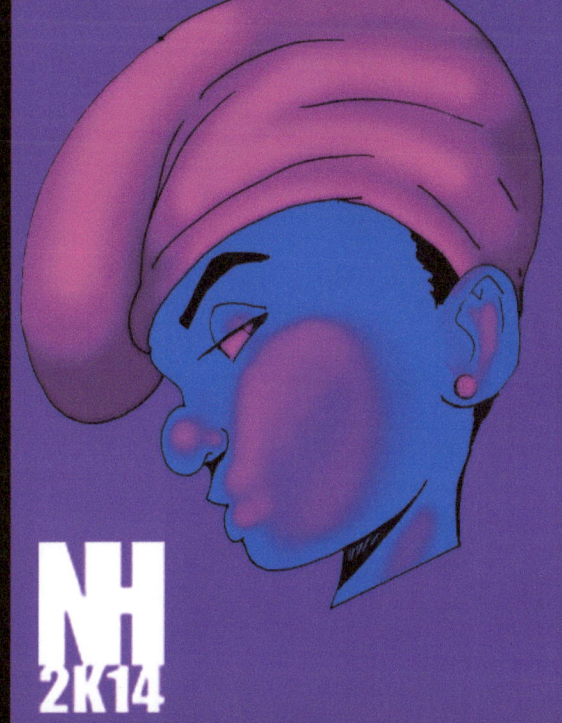
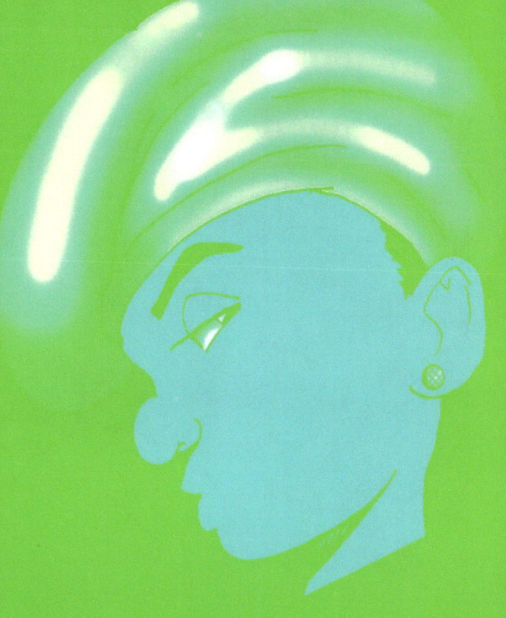

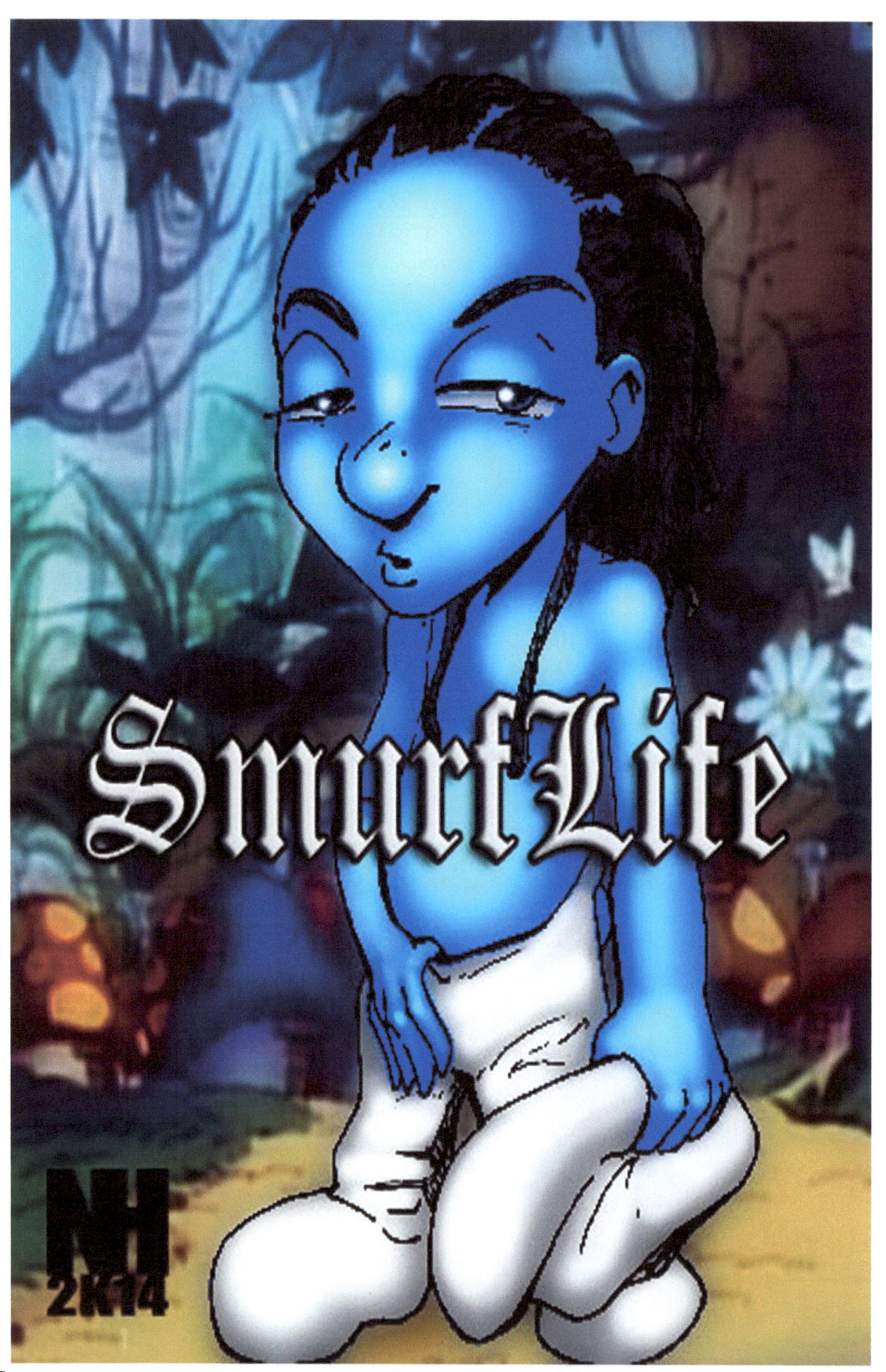

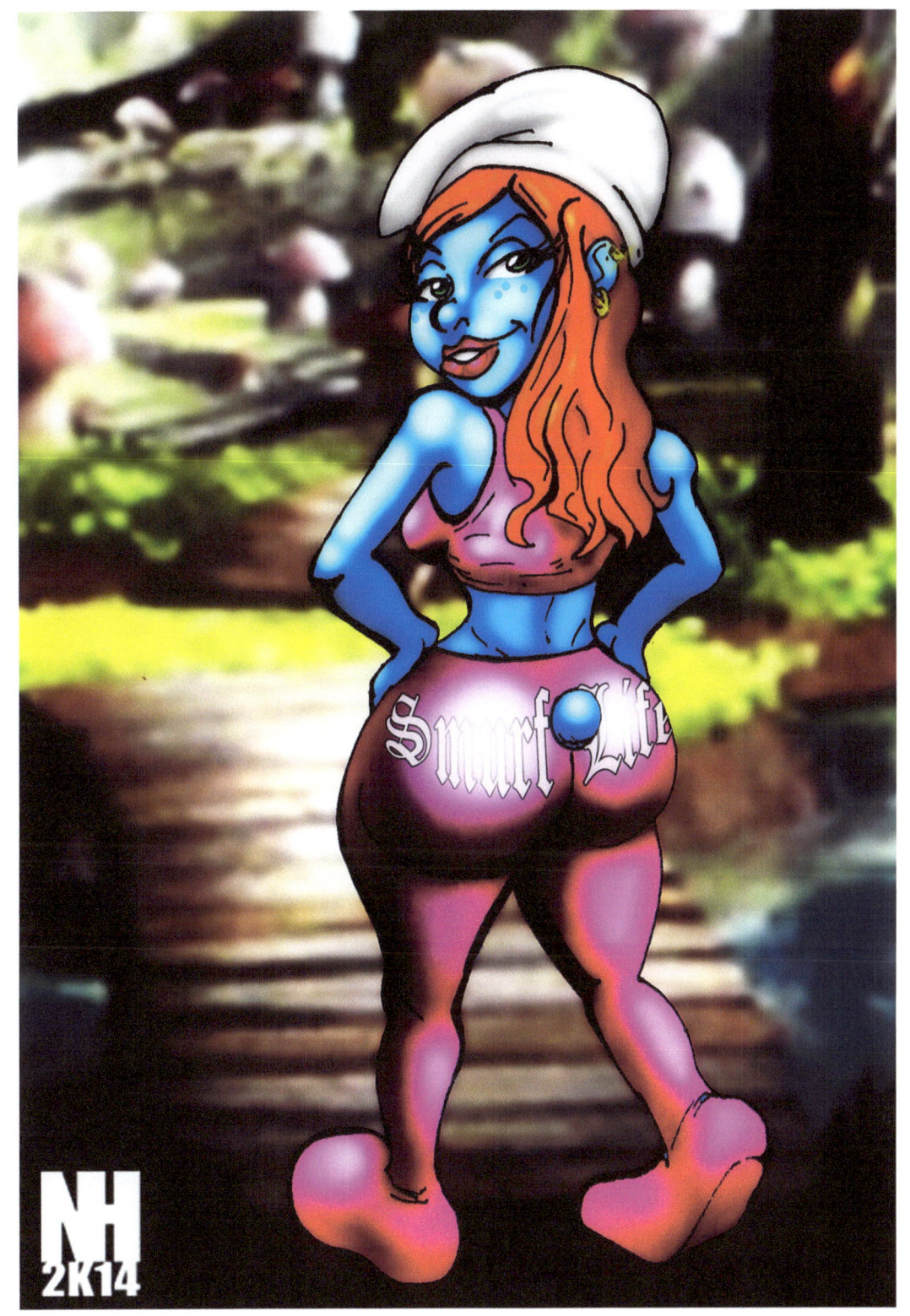

27

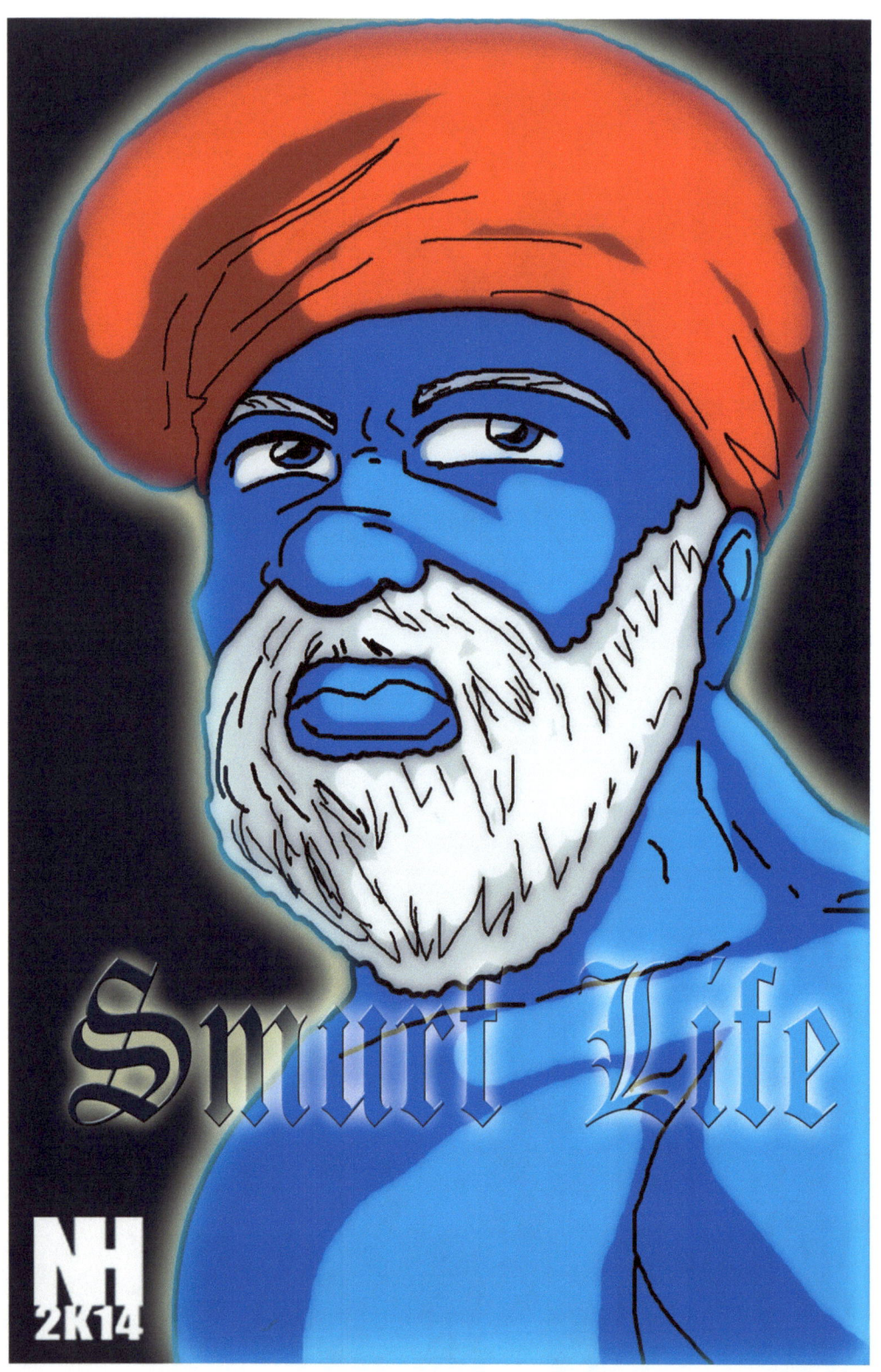

28

The next four pieces are Hip-Hop renditions of some Bad guys from toons of the best decade, the 1980s. If you want to buy these on a shirt, poster etc. just contact me norv1408@gmail.com
SUBJECT: 80s stuff

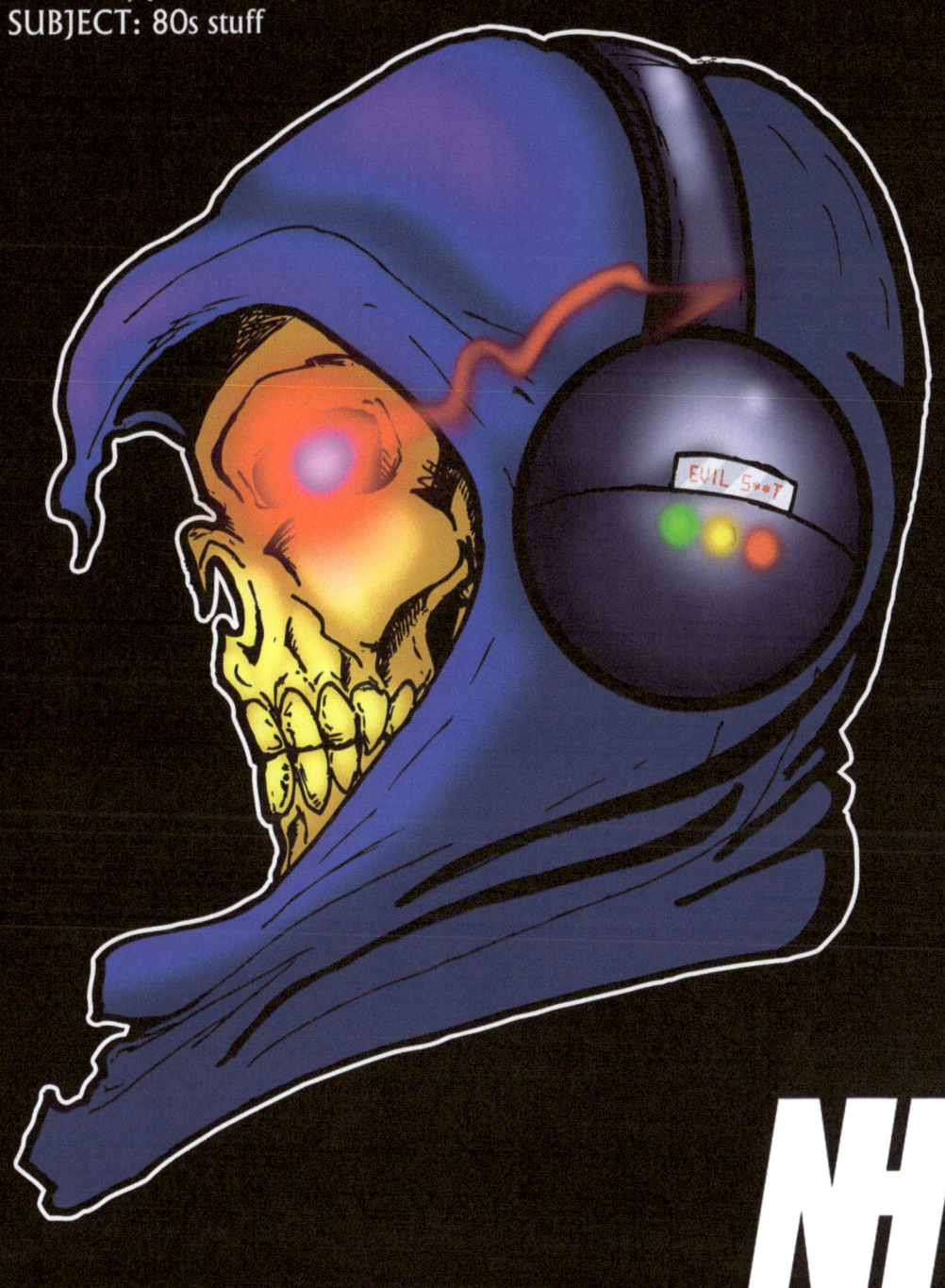

NH
2K16
29

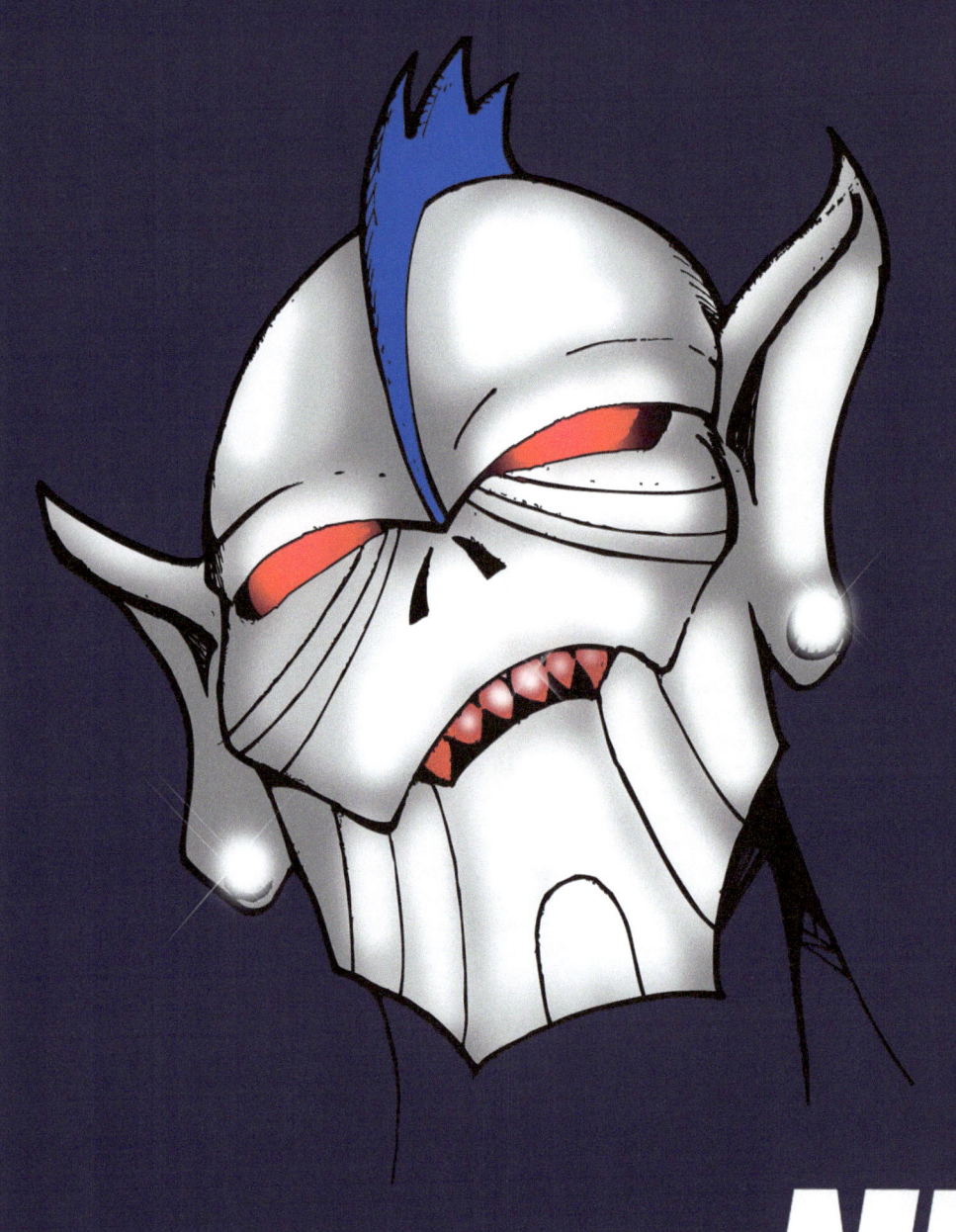

NH
2K16

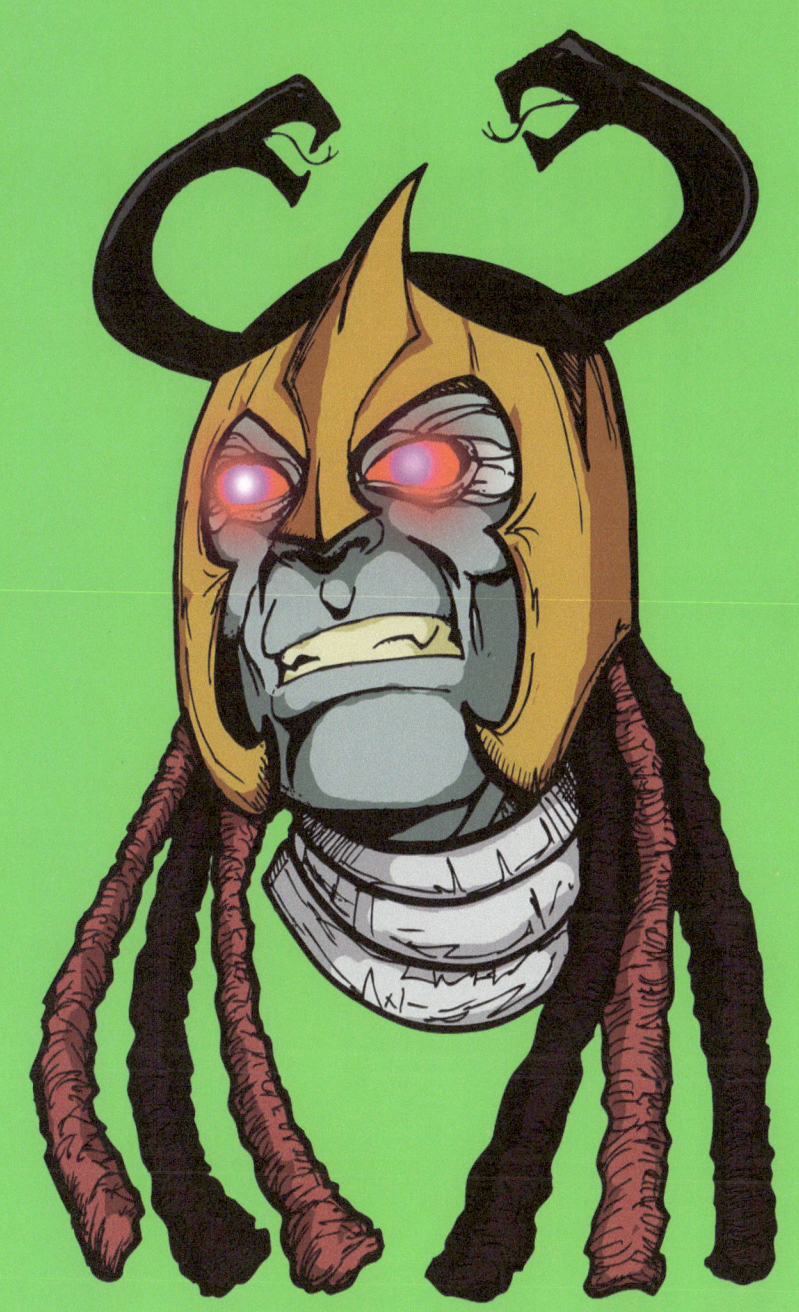

NH
2K16

31

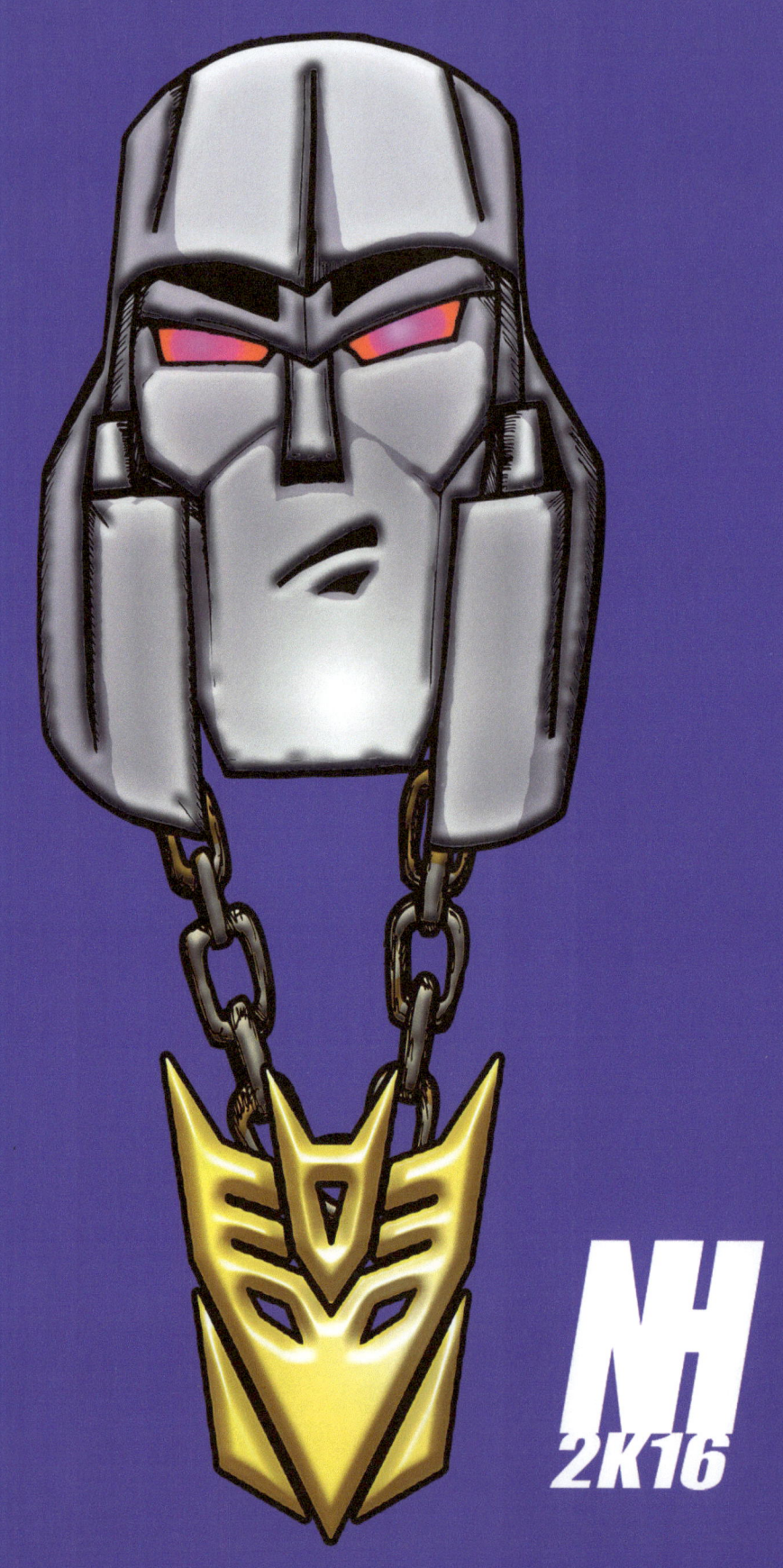

NH
2K16

32

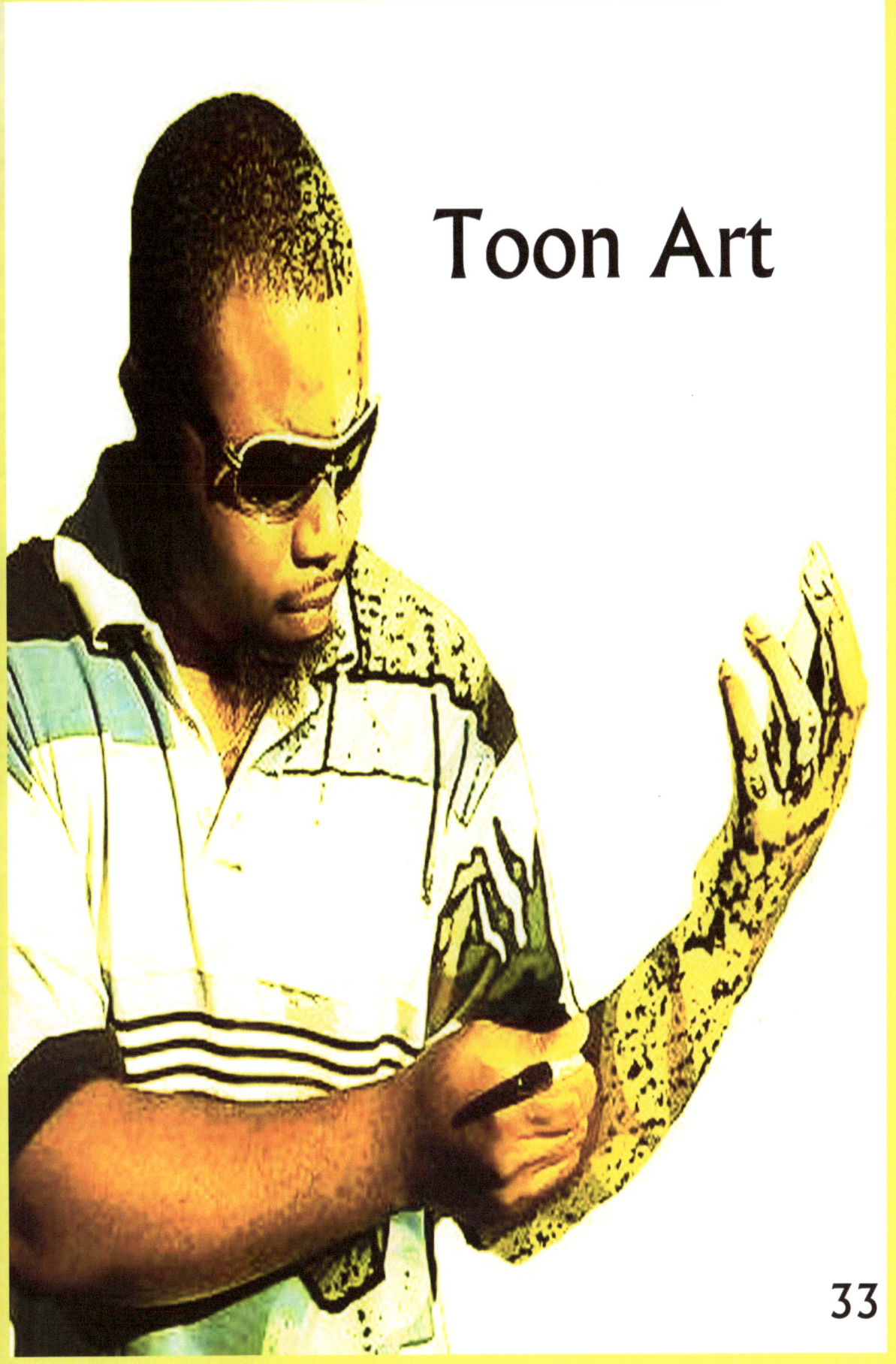

Toon Art

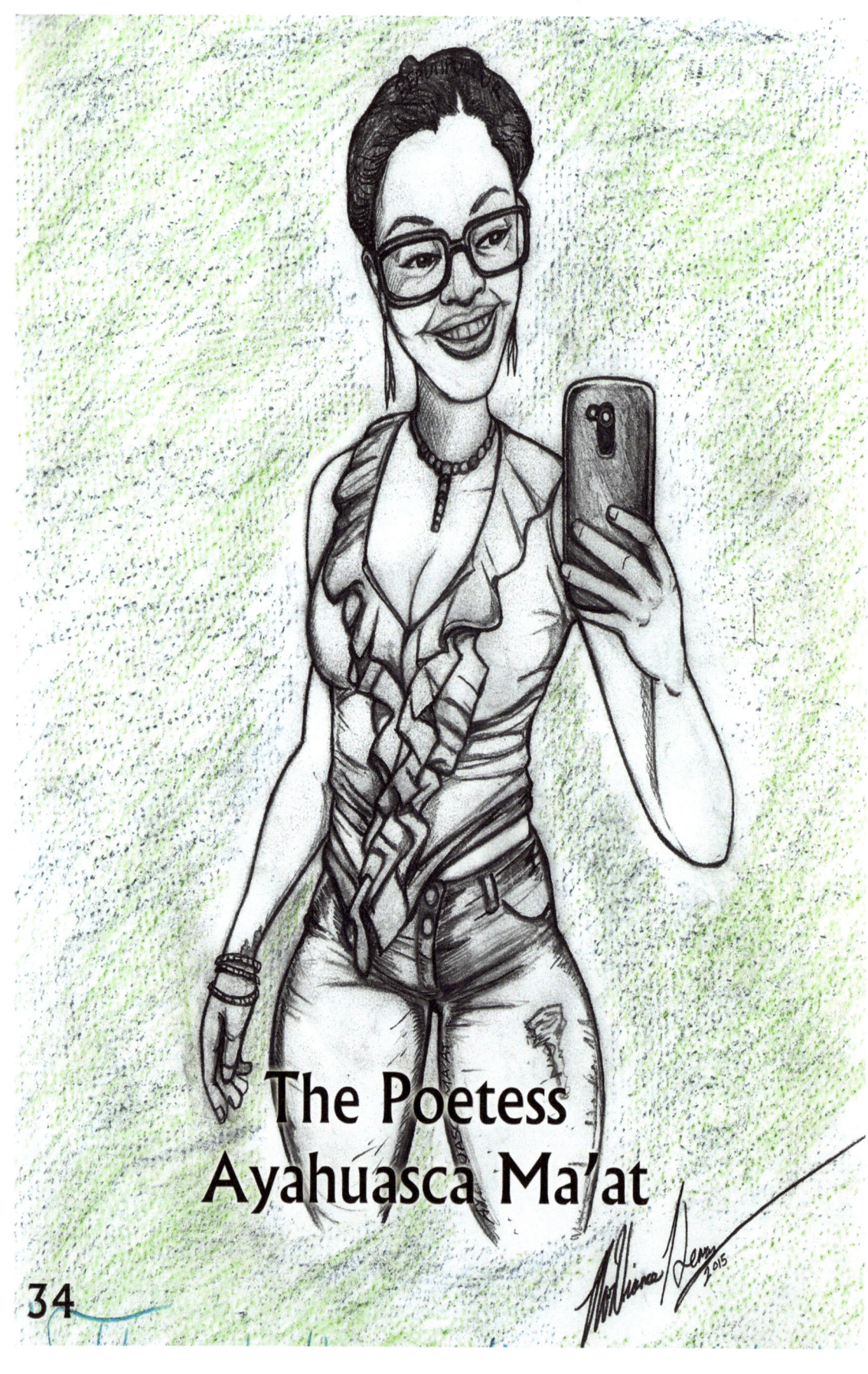

The Poetess
Ayahuasca Ma'at

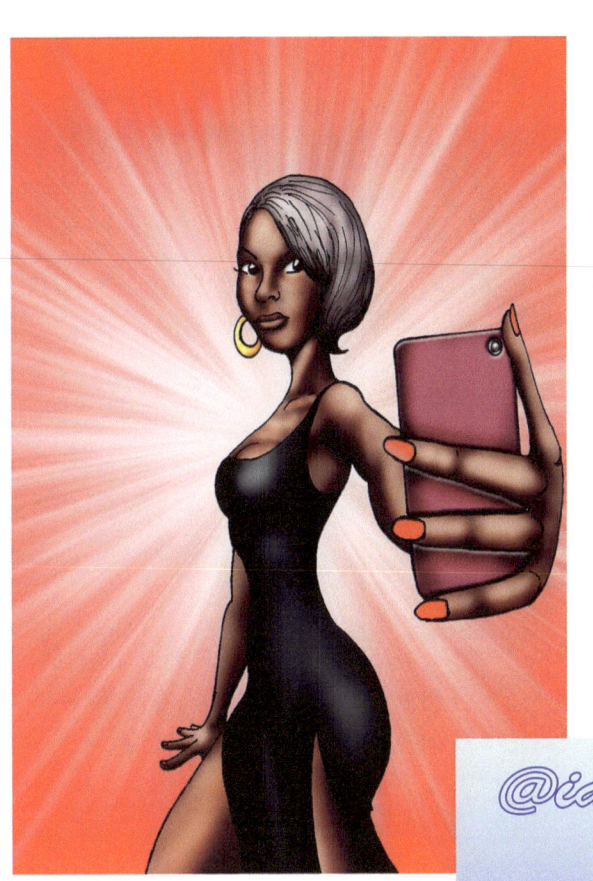

Art of
Socialite
Bo Talley

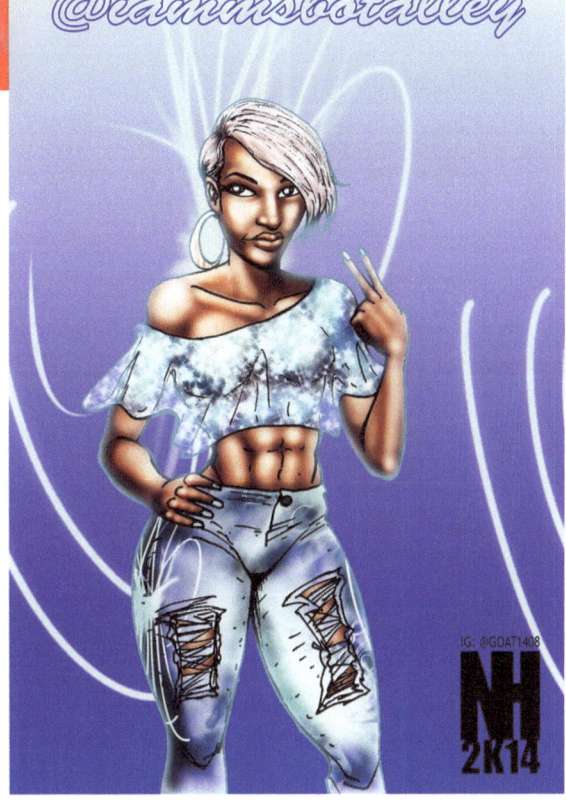

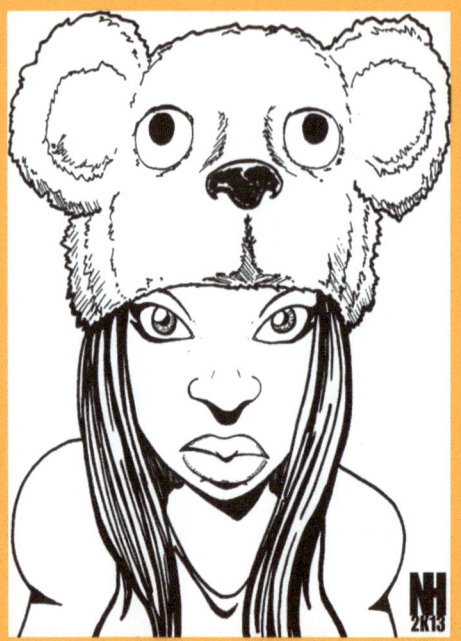

Jewels Andrea of The FountNHead

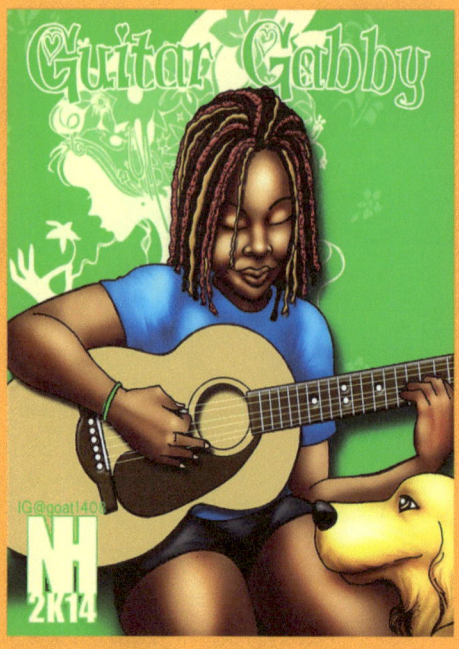

Guitar Gabby and her dog Angel
(RIP Angel, passed Dec 2015)

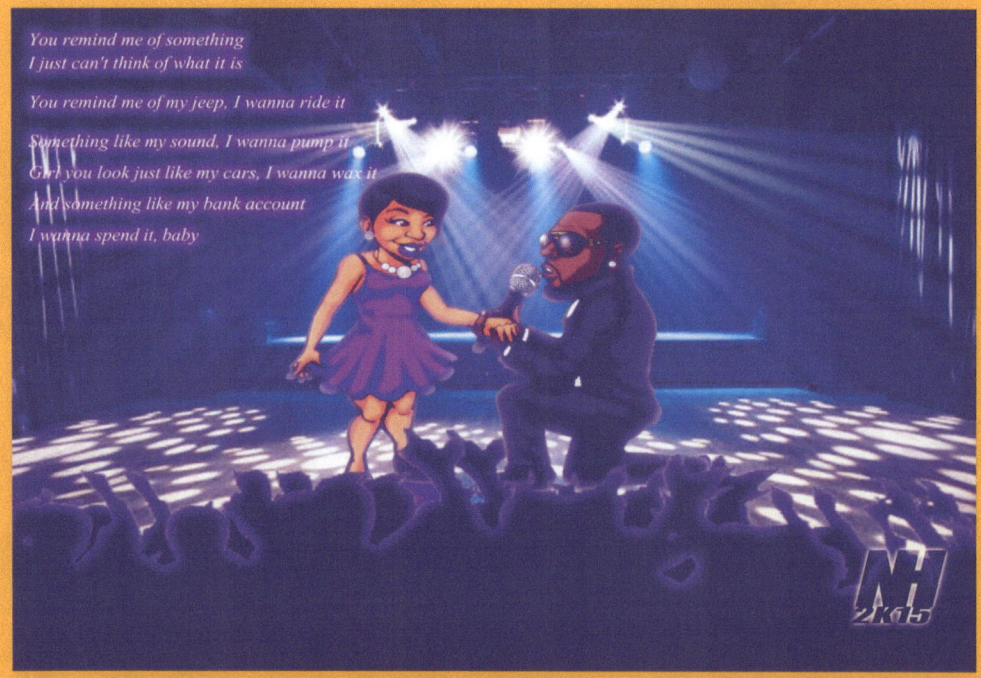

My cousin Shica, being swooned by her lifetime favorite singer, R. Kelly.

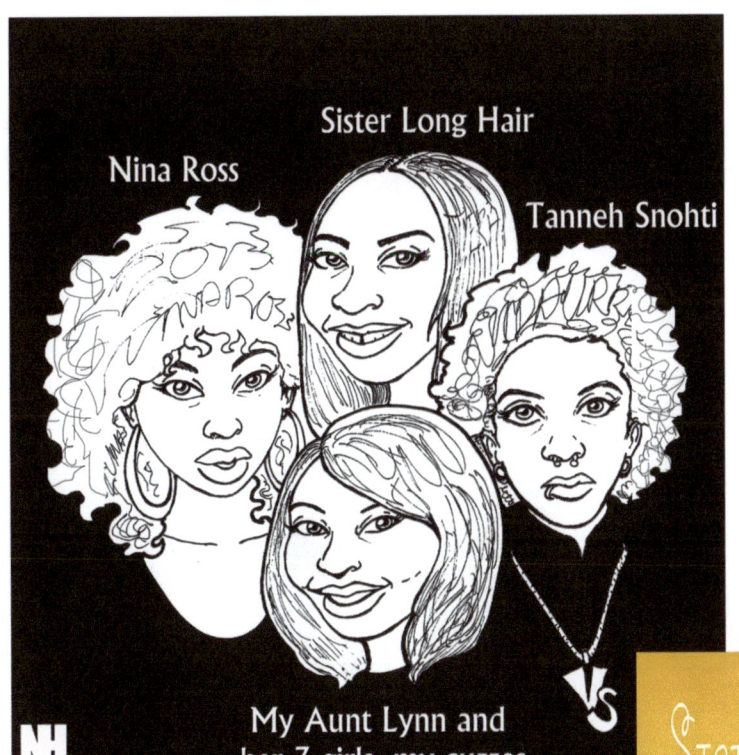

Sister Long Hair

Nina Ross

Tanneh Snohti

My Aunt Lynn and her 3 girls, my cuzzes

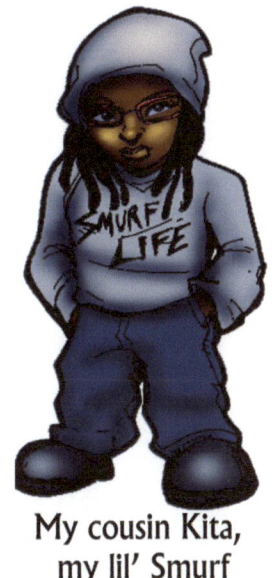

My cousin Kita, my lil' Smurf

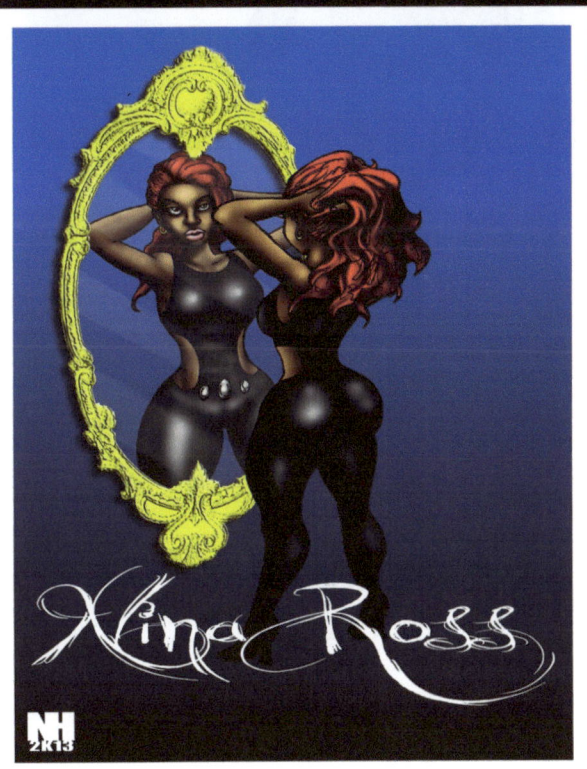

Nina Ross

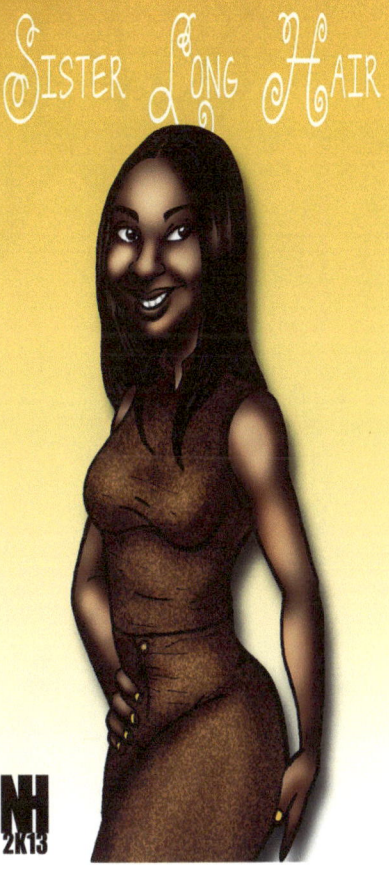

Sister Long Hair

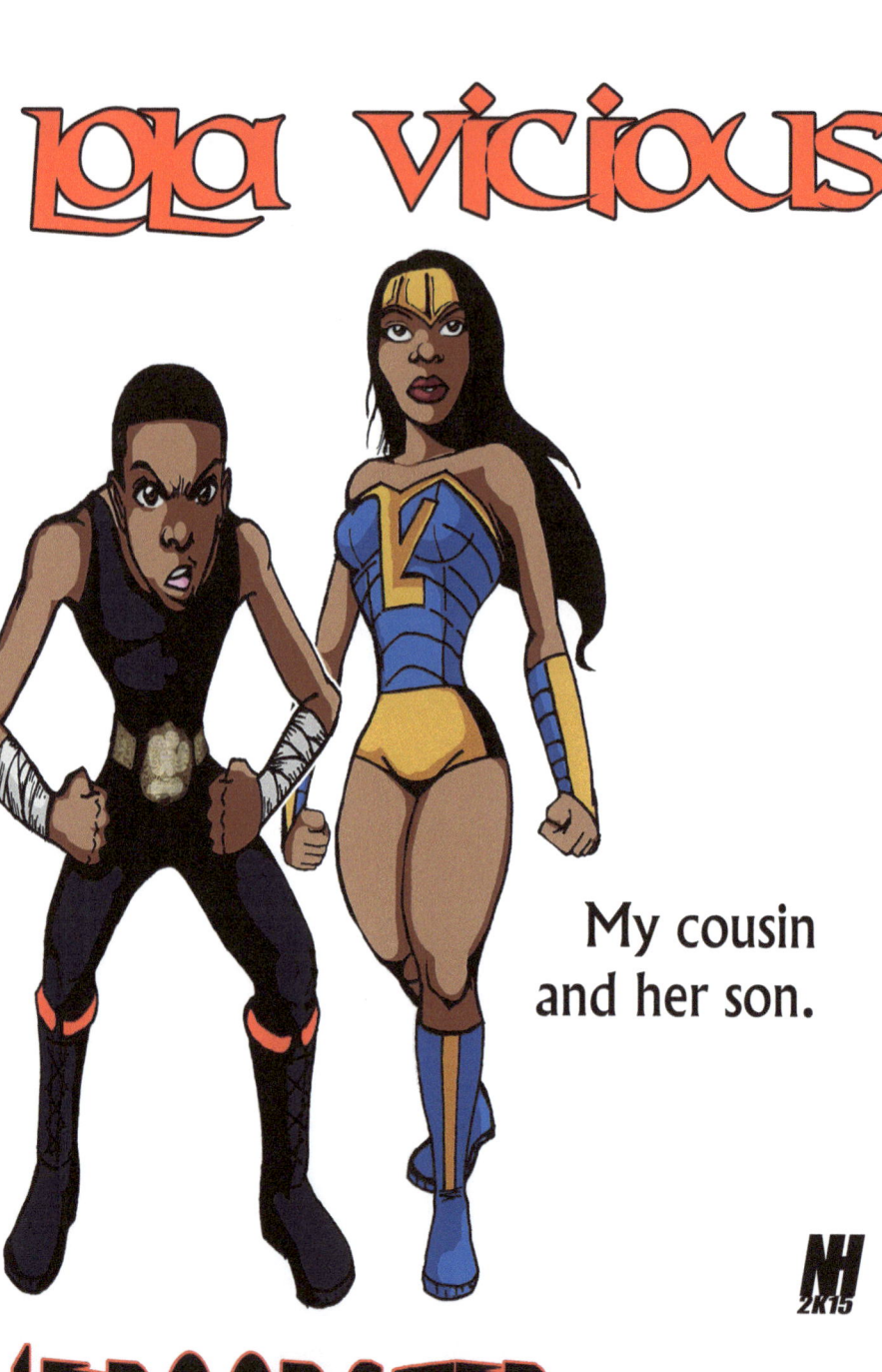

LOLA VICIOUS

My cousin
and her son.

THE DOOBSTER

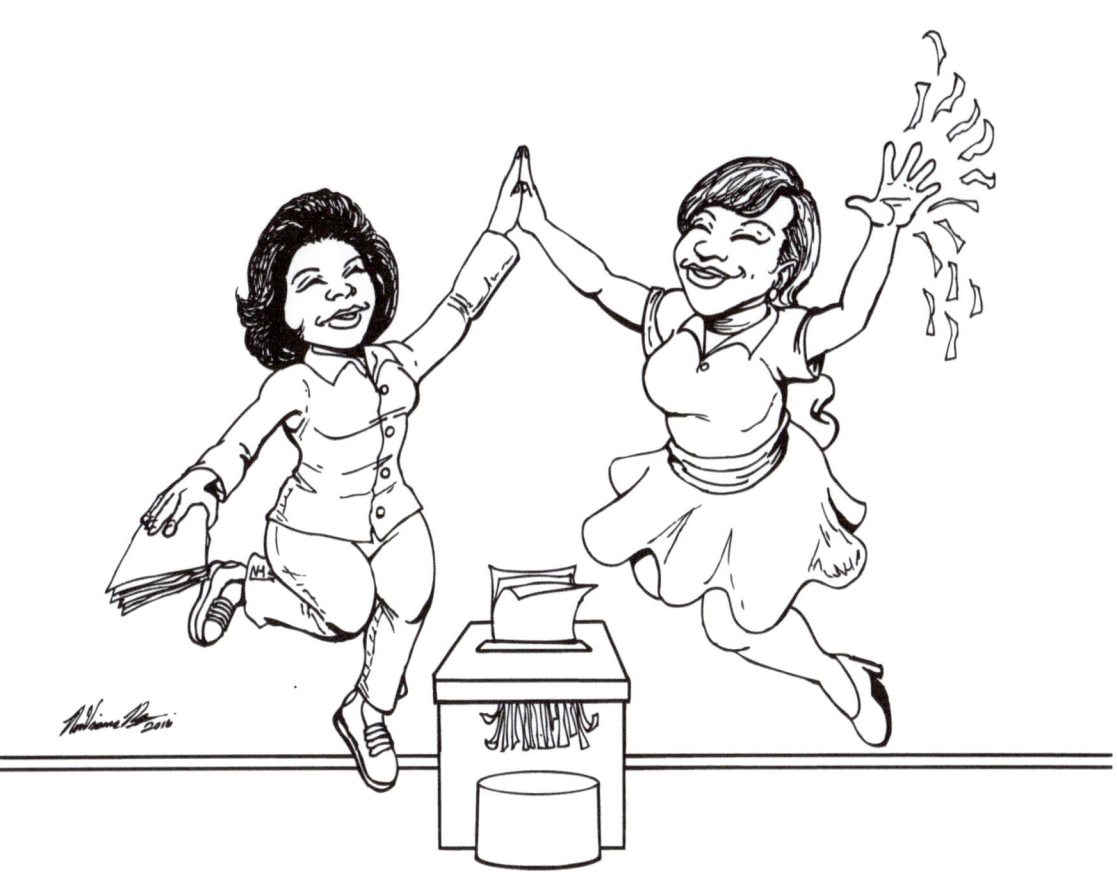

Man, talk about a time jump!!! Chances are you're reading this before you read Page 49. Allow me to explain, I'm from the future, well not your future, but the future of the guy who wrote the next ten pages, lol. Anyhoo, At this point I spent over 12 hours getting this book together, and I have only three pages left!!! This page, Page 40 and the last page, Page 50! So when I do the Acknowledgements that will be the final version of me working on this book, lol Okay, I know I lost you, so let's talk about the pic!!! I just finished drawing this while walking the Off the Wall documentary for the second time (RIP MJ) These two exuberant ladies are Heather Hill and Tanisha Clark, two of the dopest tax women in GA. Known Heather for over 20 years now and she knows what she doing, so does Nisha! Shoutouts to A Financial Solution (tell her Norv sent you) and Clark's Tax Services (Tell her the same too)!

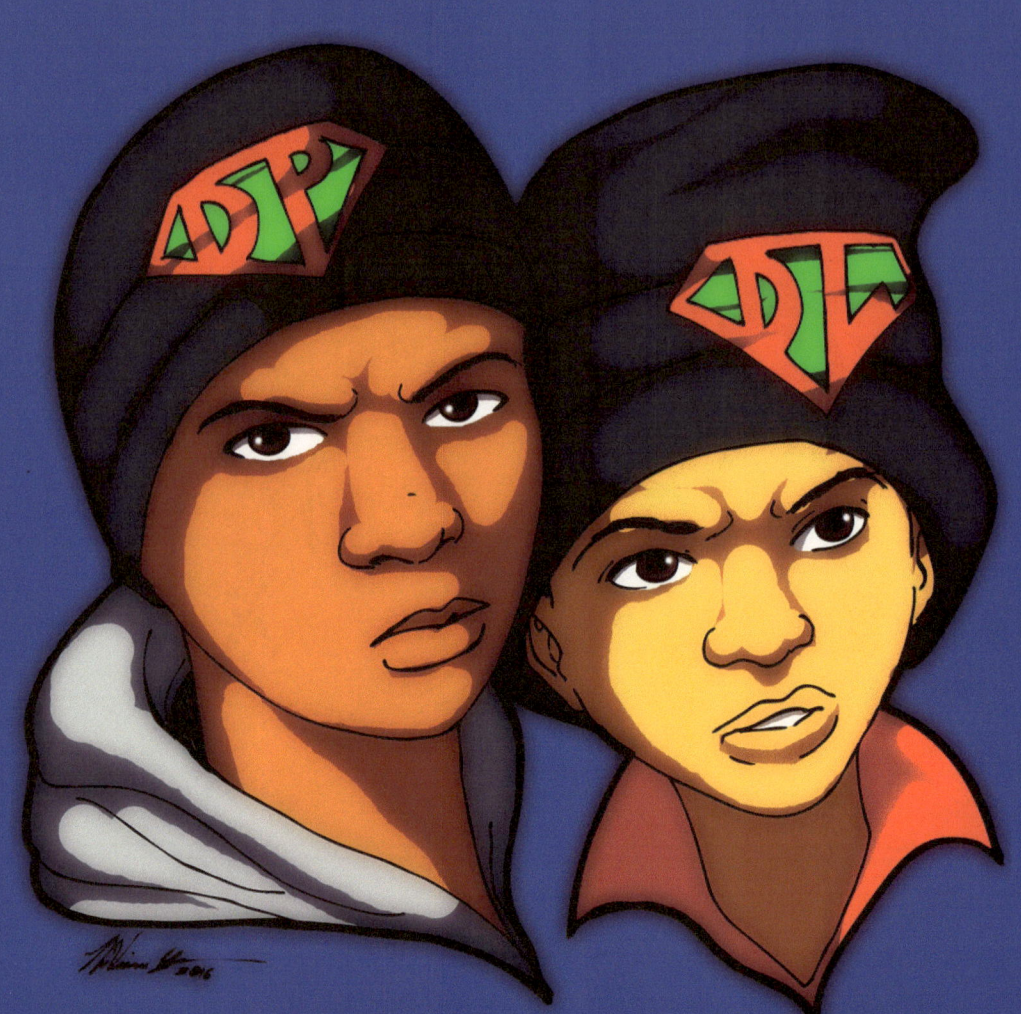

At this present time, I don't have any kids...and it weighs heavily on me. I'm my father's only son, and I want to ensure his legacy, my legacy go far into the future. The only way to do that is to find a wife who has the fortitude and strength to build with me. If I just wanted kids, I could've made them eons ago. I want a family. I want my kids to have what I had, and more. These two up here, are my great-nephews. My mom's great-grandsons. My sis made me an uncle at age 8, so I saw my niece born and grow up and now has two kids (these guys) and a daughter on the way. I want them to grow up in a world where being black is no longer a target. I gave my older g-nef that scowl because he's a GOAT like me (birthday twin). He'll need it to protect himself from the idiots of this world and his innocent fun nature. He's a big brother, so he has to get it together for his siblings, his family and most important himself. This pic is dope. Time to go write the acknowledgements. Enjoy the next ten pages leading up to it. :)

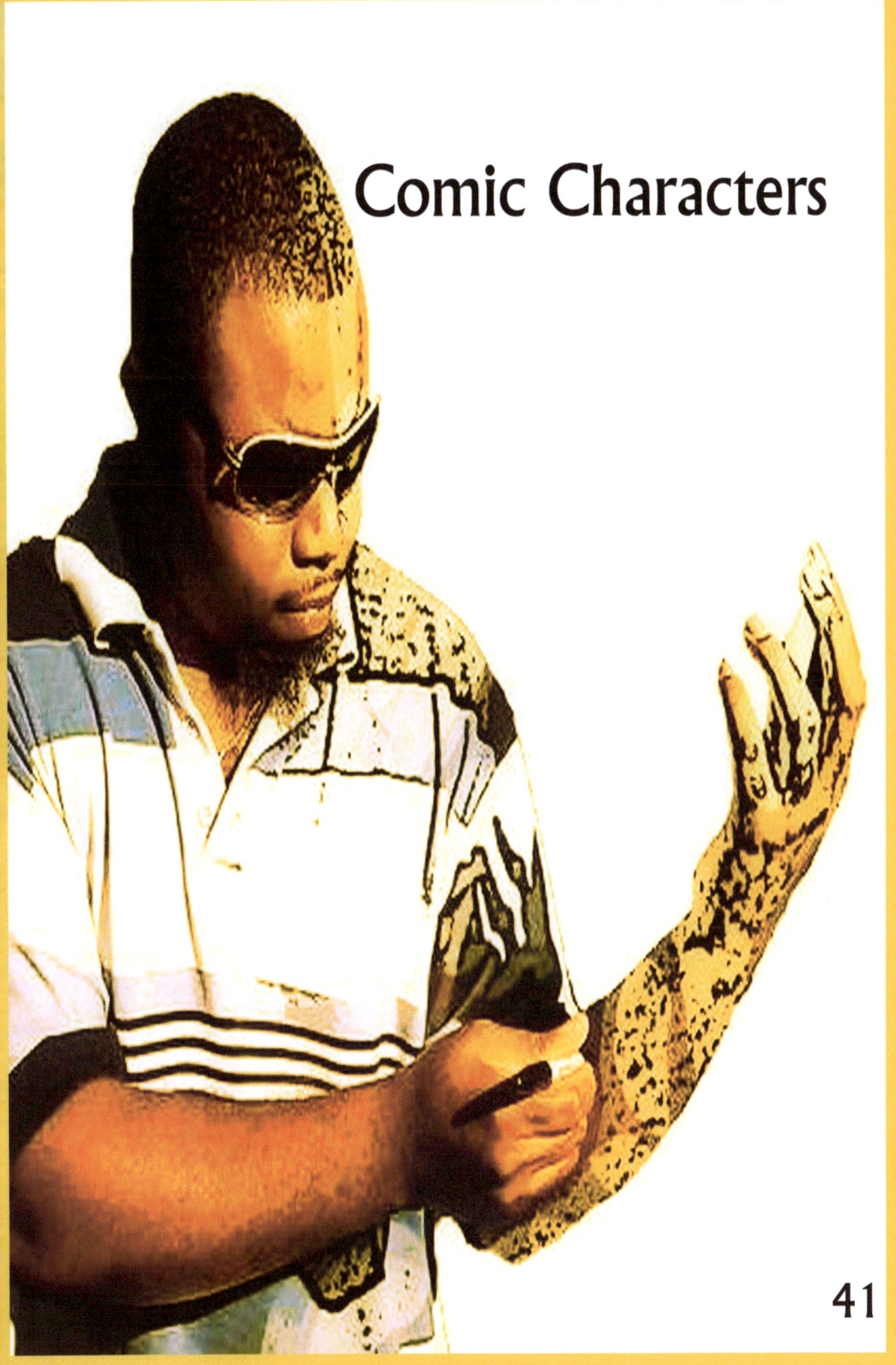

Comic Characters

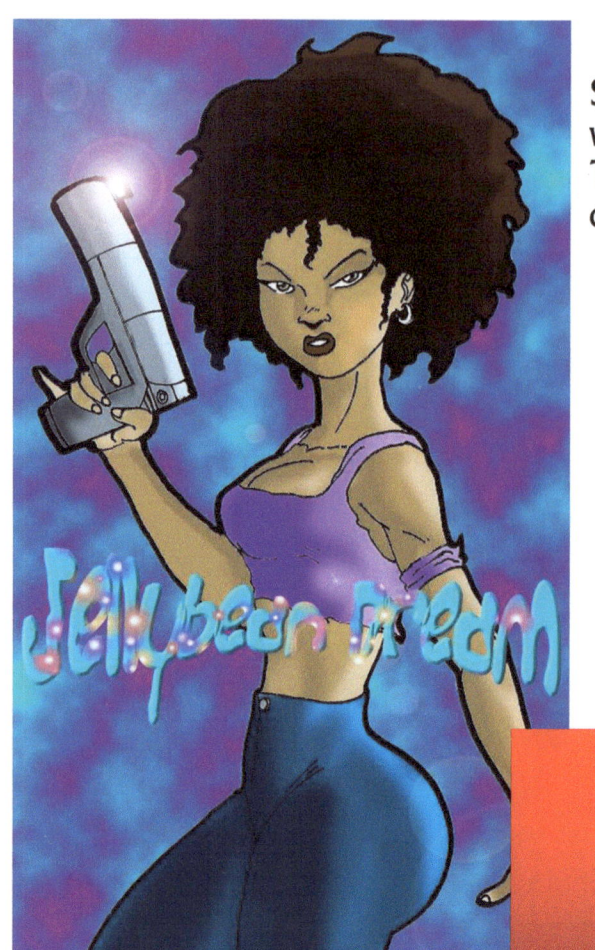

Start this section off right with Jelly of *Jellybean Dream.* This is the first picture of Jelly colored digitally.

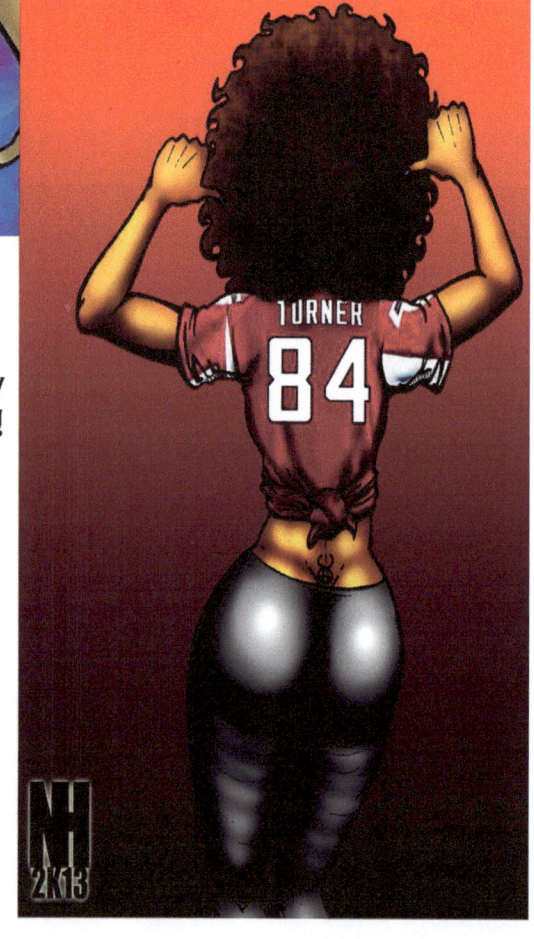

A dope pic of Jelly rocking a customized jersey of her hometown football team!

42

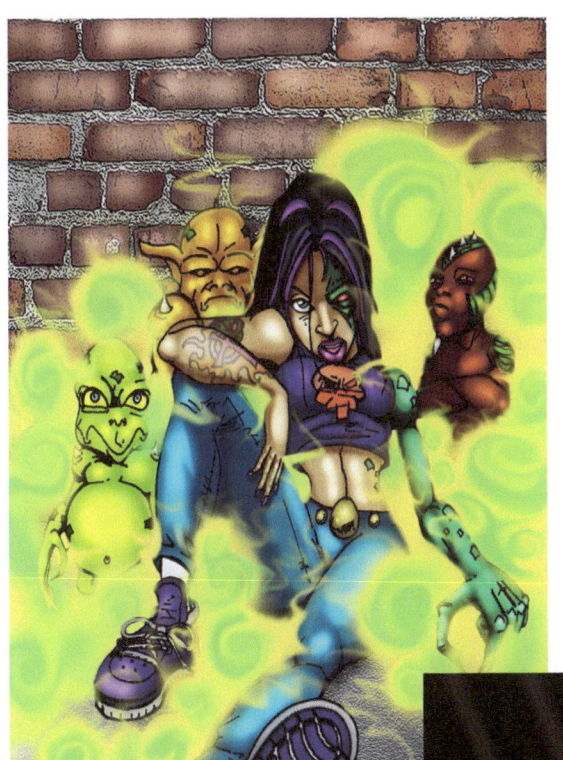

Next up is *The Force*, created by Corley Manning. Here are members of the superteam.

Facebook.com/theforcecomic

Demon Girl

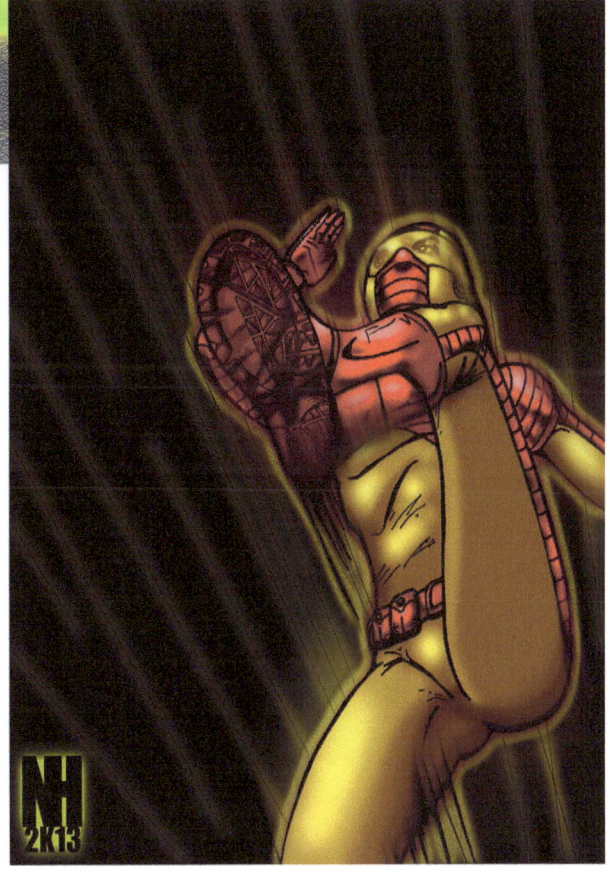

Dip

43

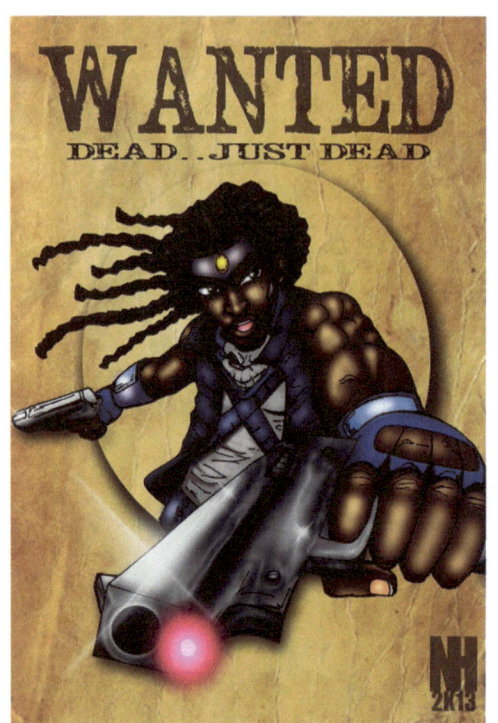
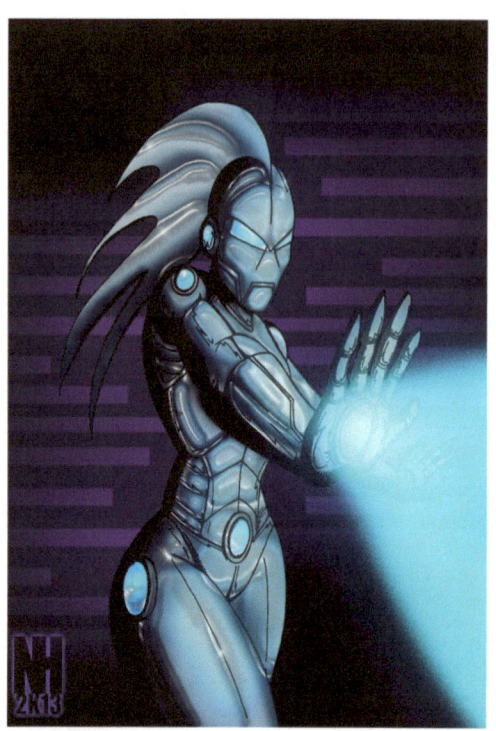
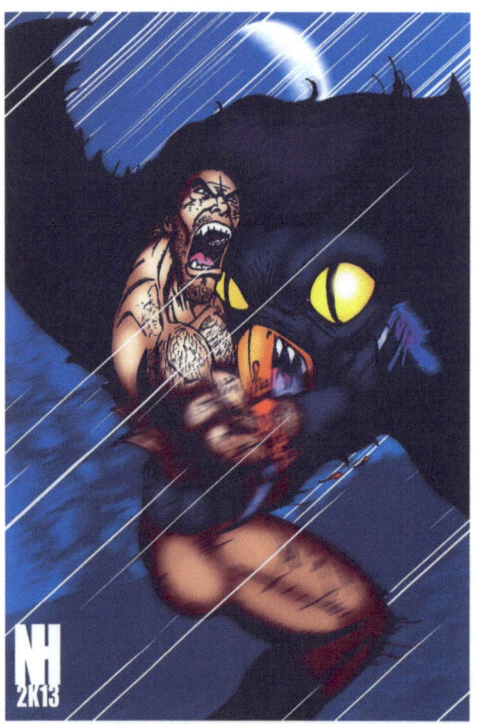
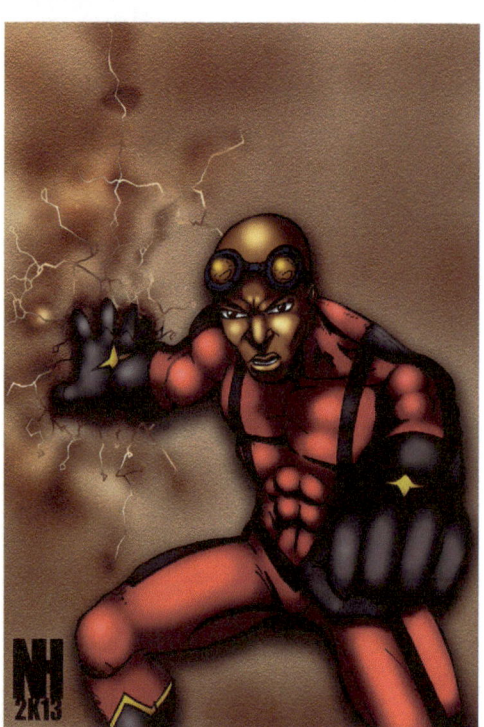

(Top L-R) Gangbanger, Iron Matrix
(Bottom L-R) Razor The Jackal, Incredible

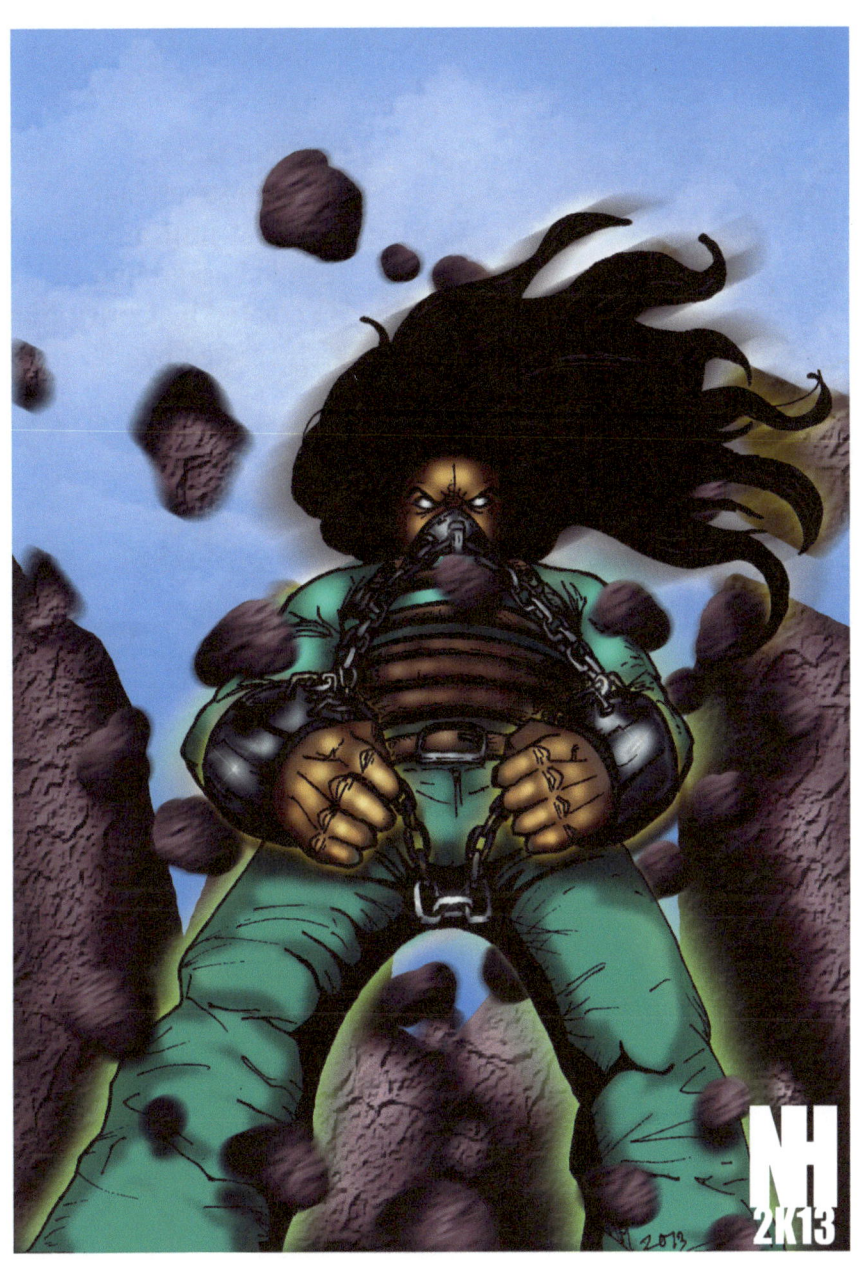

This guy is Psycho. There you have it. Get ready for The Force, coming March 15th from Urbangod Ink. To buy these pieces as posters and/or apparel contact me at norv1408@gmail.com
SUBJECT: Force Art

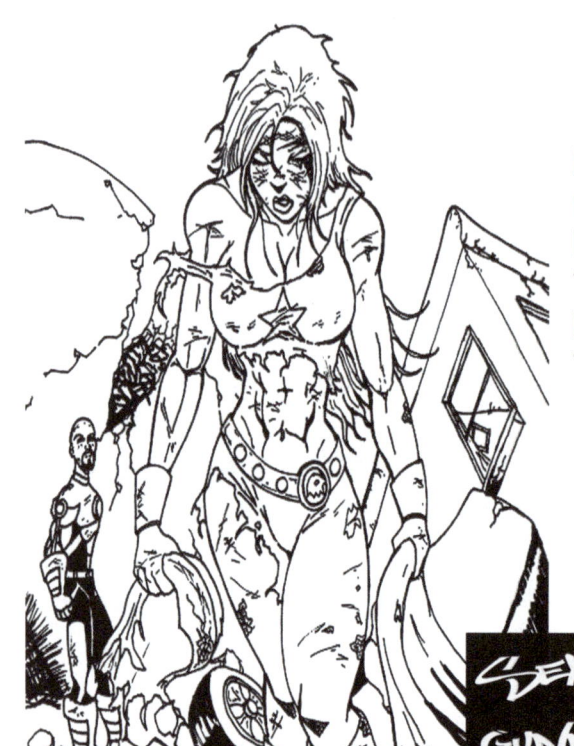

Freedom Girl
from the superteam
Legion of Justice
Tech in background.
FG created by Corley Manning
Tech created by me.

Sexi Gunner created by
Corley Manning

SEXi
GUNNER

NH
2K14

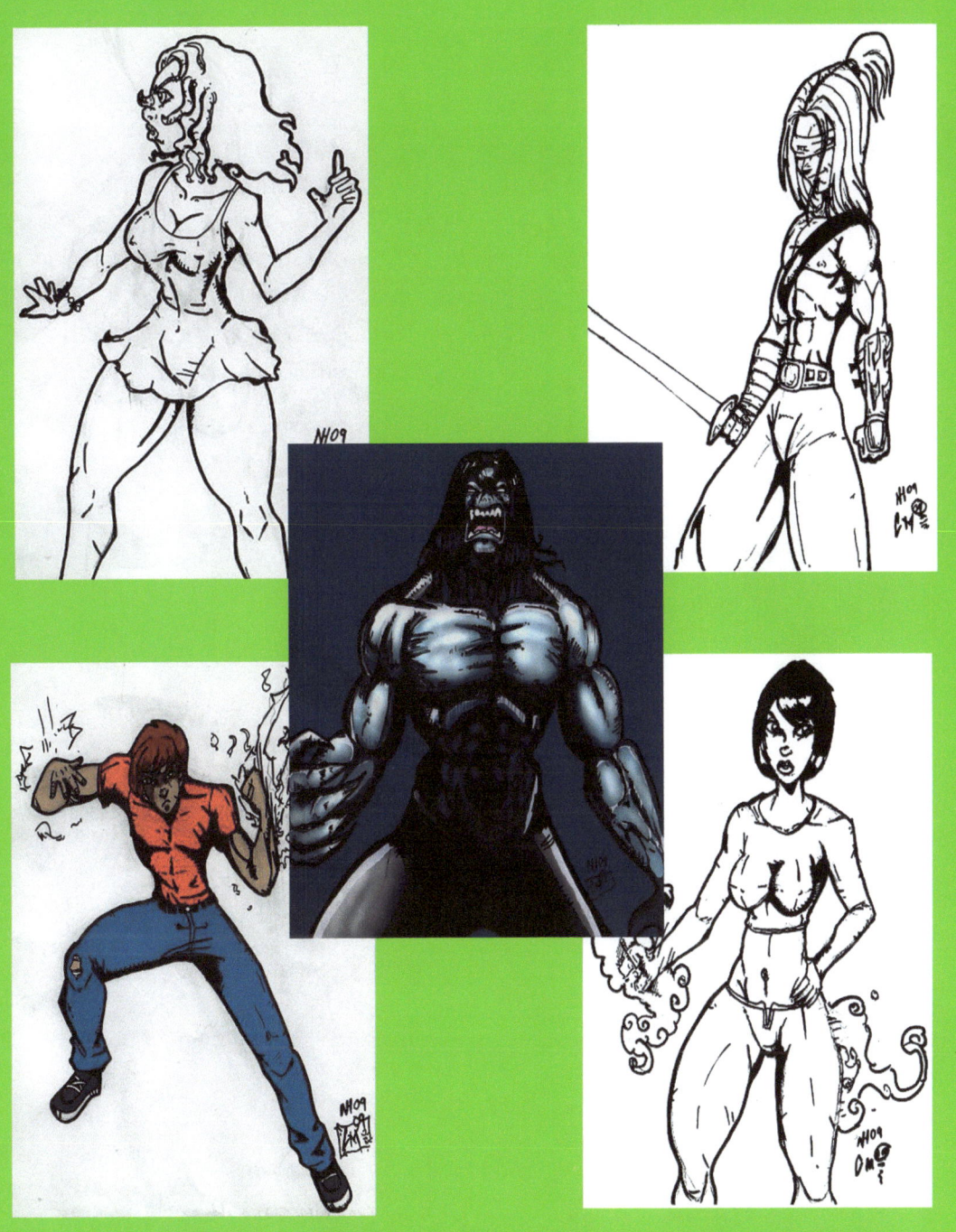

Members of the superteam known as The Society.
Who are they? Find out soon...... Pencils by me
inks and colors by Corley Manning.

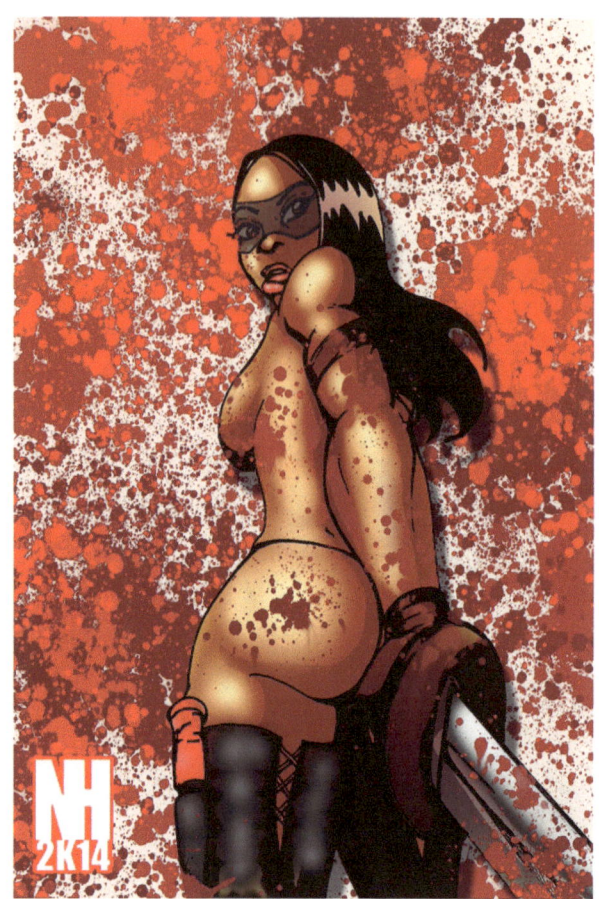

What started as a crazy idea is becoming bloody serious! From the mind of writer Cherie Johnson comes *Cherie Shinobi!*!! Get ready to cut some in 2016!

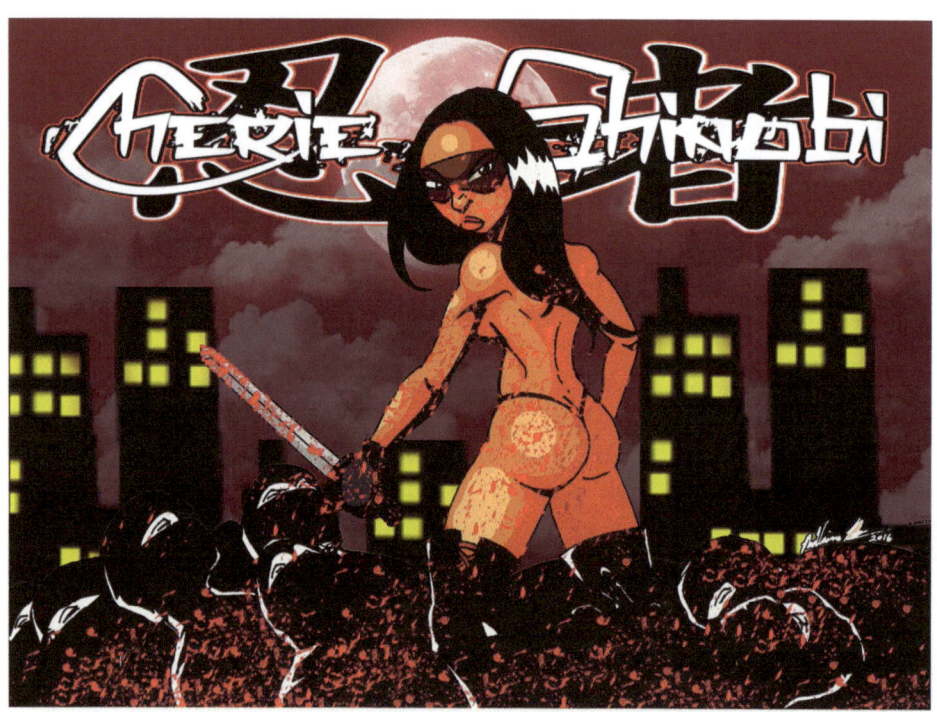

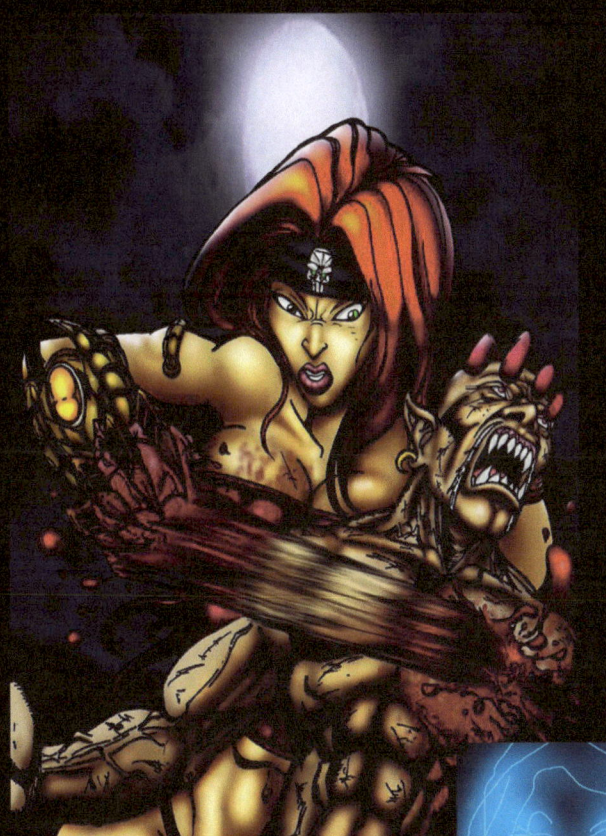

As of now I'll be in a time loop. You see, I've just put together the page you're looking at now, BUT I at my present time have not even drawn Page 39 yet! Freaky right? Of course in your present time everything is A-Ok. I can only imagine how relieved I'll be once I have put Pages 39 and 40 in their place. Page 40 is drawn but I have not scanned it in yet! Okay, enough about those pages, on to this page!!! Well, what can I say? Made these two polar opposites of each other as a teenager.

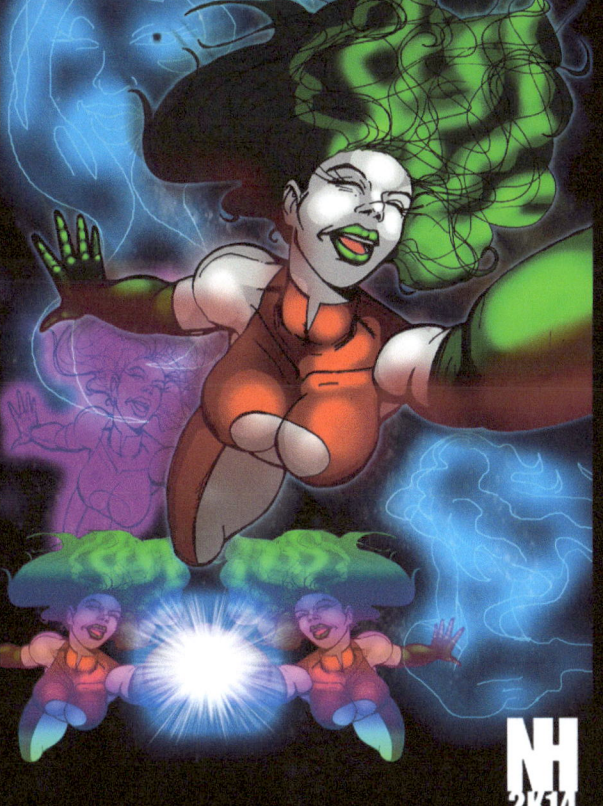

Above is Rafina Blood, a kick azz BAB that I created over 20 years ago. My friend Corley Manning revised her story in the early 2000s. To the right is possibly the strongest character I ever made, and the sweetest. She is Vertigo. and she is EVERYWHERE. Don't believe me? LOOK OVER YOUR SHOULDER!! Lol You looked, didn't you? Well onto finishing up Pages 39 and 40. You can go on ahead to the end. I'll be there eventually.

NH
2K14

Acknowledgements

Whoohoooo I made it!!!! Man, ok I had an idea about an artbook for a long time, but didn't know if I had enough work to share with you all. I don't have shelves of sketchbooks or anything like that. Because Idk, I guess I still feel like I'm not that great. Of course we as artists have those feelings all the time. So I always remind myself that I AM MY ONLY COMPETITION. I can't let what the next man or woman is doing influence what I myself do. Earlier today, I told myself I would make an artbook that would be engaging to the reader. I hope I succeeded. If you like it, let me know. If not, I'll just do it again, because I can. You can too. Live life 'til you die.
Art on this page can be purchased on society6.com/goat1408

Thanks to God for pushing me through to create this book in a 12 plus hour span, my dad for encouraging me to get it done and my mom for forever being there for me.